# THE COMPLETE
# YOGURT COOKBOOK
## BY KAREN CROSS WHYTE

ILLUSTRATED by DENNIS REDMOND

TROUBADOR PRESS ☙ SAN FRANCISCO

*For Malcolm, Kirsty and Andrew*

First Trade Paperback Edition ISBN 912300-65-5

# CONTENTS

# INTRODUCTION

Yogurt has been the staple of peasants and the delicacy of kings since antiquity. On banquet tables of the wealthy, it was used in elaborately prepared recipes, it's flavor blended with exotic Eastern spices. In its homey, plain form yogurt was an entire meal for the poor. Nomadic tribes and lords of the land had unwavering faith in yogurt's healing power. Yogurt has endured four millennia of tasting and testing.

It is only natural that yogurt, a lactic fermentation of milk, should have been discovered so many years ago. The lack of refrigeration and the unsanitary condition in which milk was stored made a natural breeding ground for bacteria, both harmful and beneficial. When milk is innoculated with one or more of the yogurt bacteria, they begin to grow and form lactic acid, killing any harmful bacteria which may have infected the milk. The three most commonly used bacteria to bring about fermentation in making yogurt today are *Lactobacillus yogurt*, *Streptococcus thermophilus* and *Lactobacillus bulgaricus*. These are used separately or combined.

The type of milk used differs from area to area as does the kind of bacteria. In the United States, cow's milk is used; in Lapland, reindeer and mare's milk; in Bulgaria, cow, sheep and goat's milk are commonly used. Buffalo milk is used in Armenia, as well as cow's and goat's milk. Even soy bean milk may be used to make yogurt! The flavor varies with the type of milk used, the type of food the animal providing the milk eats and the method employed in making the yogurt.

The consistency of each type of yogurt also varies. Cow's milk produces a dense yogurt. Buffalo milk makes a very rich curd. *Kaelder* milk (cellar milk) of Norway is a ropy, alcoholic milk, while *taettle* of Scandinavia has a slimy consistency. In *kefer* and *koumiss* of Southern Russia, the culture used produces a highly acid, potently alcoholic brew. Effervescent like champagne, it keeps out the cold and stimulates, but has an exceedingly strong flavor. Ass's milk produces a fine curd and is easily digested by infants. The acidity of yogurt is another variable depending largely on the bacillus and the type of process used to make it. In spite of all these differences each yogurt is "the real thing."

Today our commercial yogurt can be bought in supermarkets almost everywhere in the United States. It comes in a variety of sizes, flavors and brands, many with a low butter fat. It is available either solid or stirred. The stirred yogurt is usually labeled "Swiss style." Yogurt has come a long way from a goatskin bag and the old earthenware vessel, covered with a bit of old sack, sitting in the sun fermenting. Modern dairies process yogurt in sterilized, stainless steel 40 quart cans with temperatures controlled thermostatically. Although yogurt is mass produced and sanitarily packaged, it has emerged into the twentieth century basically the same creamy, refreshing and nourishing food it was four thousand years ago.

# THE HISTORY OF YOGURT

Any of the middle Eastern or Balkan Countries would be proud to claim the origin of a food that has played such an important part in the diets of so many people, though none can be singled out. The name "yogurt," which we use in the United States, is of Turkish origin. Bearing many other names, yogurt was eaten in the ancient world from the Arab countries through the Middle East to Central Asia and Southern Europe. Today, yogurt is a universal food.

In India, about 2,500 years ago, yogis formed rules for eating and drinking, cautioning their followers against eating sour foods. The only exception was milk. *Dahi* (yogurt in India) the yogis said, was "food for the gods," especially when eaten with honey.

Galen, a famous Greek physician known as "Wonder-Worker" in the 2nd century A.D., claimed yogurt had a "beneficial purifying effect on the bilious and burning stomach." Galen also said that milk taken straight from the cow had a burning quality, but fermented milk did not. Scientists today know that yogurt is far more easily digested than milk. Over ninety percent of yogurt is digestible in one hour compared to thirty percent in milk.

The Bulgars, wandering hordes from Asia, came to Europe (Bulgaria) from Asia in the 7th century. They settled in the Balkans around 679, bringing yogurt with them. In the same century a treatise was published in Damascus, entitled "The Great Explanation of the Power of the Elements and Medicine." Some of the most learned physicians of Greece, Arabia, Persia, Syria and

India contributed to this work, which recommended yogurt for soothing, refreshing and regulating the intestinal tract, as well as for "strengthening the stomach."

Genghis Khan fed his vast army on yogurt during their long marches through the Mongolian and Persian Empires when no other food was obtainable. When meat was available, he used yogurt as a meat preservative.

Legend tells of the ill and aging French Emperor, Francis I, regaining his health when given a "secret formula" by a man who brought it all the way from Constantinople. Impressed by their Emperor's recovery, the court physicians paid thousands of francs for the formula. This potion turned out to be a form of yogurt made from goat's milk. And that, according to legend, is how yogurt became known in France as *lait de la vie eternelle*, "the milk of long life."

Mahatma Gandhi, concerned about how to feed the starving people of his native India, made a study of foods, many not included in any books on nutrition. He learned to make use of food that might ordinarily be thrown away and to prepare salad with green leaves not usually eaten. Gandhi made these studies so the poor might improve their diet. His book, "Diet Reform," a collection of notes and articles he wrote on nutrition, devoted an entire chapter to the merits of yogurt.

Without a doubt, the man most responsible for introducing yogurt to the Western world was a Russian born professor named Ilya Metchnikoff. His research in physiology at the Pasteur Institute in Paris won the doctor the Nobel Prize in 1908. Metchnikoff's books, *The Prolongation of Life*, *The Nature of Man*, and *Old Age*, reveal his concern for what he considered to be premature aging in humans. Research led him to investigate yogurt and coincidentally to discover some amazing facts about the Bulgarians, then among the poorest people of the world. They ate yogurt, but were deprived of many other foods considered necessary for good health. He found at the time of his study that there were 1,600 Bulgarians over the age of one hundred out of every million compared to only eleven Americans per million. During his investigation, Metchnikoff identified and isolated the bacilli that created yogurt, thus making it possible to process the food on a large scale.

Metchnikoff found that bacteria putrefied in the large intestine and reabsorbtion of these decaying organisms poisoned the body. He believed that the lactic acid in yogurt would rid the large intestine of these harmful bacteria. Not only was the large intestine purified, but as a bonus yogurt manufactured generous amounts of B vitamins in the digestive tract which were absorbed and distributed throughout the body. The professor concluded that yogurt was the magical food responsible for the long lived Bulgarians. He gave yogurt the label "health food," stating that if a man ate yogurt regularly, he would live to be one hundred fifty years old.

After consumming large quantities of yogurt every day for twenty years, Metchnikoff died at the age of seventy one, dampening the enthusiasm of his followers. Fortunately one of his followers, a Spanish businessman, Issac Carasso, did not lose interest.

Impressed with the Russian's investigation, Carasso obtained cultures from Bulgaria and the Pasteur Institute with which he manufactured a yogurt culture to be sold through pharmacies. He extended his market to France, and later to the United States. When World War II broke out, Carasso's son Daniel came to the United States bringing his father's precious culture with him. Daniel started a small yogurt factory to supply ghettos of Arabs, Turks and Greeks around New York. The younger Carasso took a partner, Joe Metzger, and the two men set about introducing yogurt to the masses. They dropped Metchnikoff's obsessive claim that yogurt is a "health food," advertising it instead as "a food that tastes good." The psychology of the new approach assured the success of yogurt in the United States.

There were other paths yogurt followed to reach America. One of the first journeys started when a group of Trappist monks migrated to Canada. They were accompanied by a cow to provide milk for their yogurt which was made daily on the long voyage. In their new Canadian settlement, the monks built a monastery and organized the Oka Agriculture School. In 1932, Dr. Jose Maria Rosell and Professor Gustave Toupin founded the Rosell Institute, and the Trappist monks permitted them to locate it in their Oka Agriculture School. The main purpose of the Rosell Institute was to produce cultures used in the manufacture of cultured milk products.

In 1939, Richard Tille of Chicago obtained a franchise from the Rosell Institute for the distribution of Rosell yogurt culture throughout the United States. Tille formed the Continental Yogurt Company to produce and promote commercial yogurt and its culture for home production. In 1942 the business moved to Los Angeles to become the Yami Yogurt Company. The cultures they use are still obtained from the Rosell Institute in Canada.

There are now many commercial brands of yogurt on the market representing dairies large and small. As the demand increases, these companies constantly and competitively improve the quality, flavor and variety of yogurt products.

Recent successful experiments in the freeze-drying processes have dramatically changed the life of yogurt. Historically, yogurt has been a poor traveler. Its manufacture was limited to the area Nomads traveled with their animals. They made and carried their supply in goat skin bags. Fresh milk was required to make fresh yogurt every few days in order to preserve the bacillus. The introduction of refrigeration prolonged the yogurt life span to a couple of weeks. Now, freeze-dried strains of lactic bacteria can travel around the world without loss of quality. These cultures will remain active for many months, even years.

# YOGURT FOLKLORE

There are endless claims of healthful benefits derived from a steady diet of yogurt. Some are made from controlled scientific investigations, others from generations of use. Health faddists and nutritionists named yogurt as one of the "top five" health producing foods. As to its basic food value, there is no controversy. Yogurt has about the same nutritional value as milk, the almost perfect food. Fermentation of sugar into acid, alcohol or gas causes yogurt to have a slightly lower sugar content. The debatable element in yogurt is the value of the live bacteria to the body. This living organism is what changes milk into yogurt, turning "straw into gold." Perhaps some of the colorful lore surrounding yogurt will be found to have some validity.

It is said that in ancient Persia, a woman's worth was measured by the amount of *mast* her prospective husband could buy with her dowry. A Persian mother knew the worth of *mast* in a more aesthetic way. She included this form of yogurt in her daughter's daily diet to give her clear skin and sparkling eyes. She also used it as a soothing ointment for sunburn. The future bride was urged to use *mast* as a facial to keep her eternal Oriental youth and beauty. Writer Linda Clark instructs her modern American readers to mix yogurt and strawberries in a blender and apply the mixture as a cosmetic mask. Yogurt facials have a bleaching action, good for toning down freckles. The logic of this theory and the Persian lore can be explained. The high protein, calcium and acid content of yogurt is very beneficial to the skin.

The Mongolian warrior of Marco Polo's day, known for his hardiness and endurance, spent his leisure hours sipping *koumiss* and keeping his wife or wives (sometimes 60) happy. He depended heavily on this alcoholic form of yogurt, with it's slow intoxicating effect, to relax his war weary nerves and nourish his body. This virile nomad believed that *koumiss* would restore his thinning hair, and in times of peace, tighten his sagging stomach muscles, keep him trim and prolong his life. His faith in *koumiss* may have been well founded considering that he survived chiefly on milk products and meat, with an occasional treat of wild vegetables.

India has recognized for years *dahi's* value as a cure for hangovers. Although generally a teetotaling nation itself, she nevertheless offers this remedy to less temperate nations. For the morning after, Indians recommend *dahi* plain or thinned with water as a beverage. They claim *dahi* will induce sleep and calm the nerves. It even has "a soothing effect on hysterical subjects," they maintain. Nationally known nutritionist, Adelle Davis, states that a deficiency of calcium causes nerves to become tense, and insomnia is likely to follow due to the inability of the body to relax. Calcium tablets are sometimes called "lullaby pills." Yogurt is naturally rich in calcium; ninety-one percent of it is assimilable in one hour. Calcium from yogurt can readily be absorbed because it supplies both fat and lactic acid which aid in assimilation of the mineral.

The Balkan folk believe that yogurt has many therapeutic qualities for diseases caused by intestinal disorders. It is good for treatment of chronic constipation, colitis, ulcers and applied complaints. Persians are adamant in the belief that their fondness for yogurt renders them practically immune to ulcers and other stomach ailments.

According to Edouard Brochu, president of the Rosell Institute, "yogurt contains from 500,000,000 to 800,000,000 cells of lactic bacteria per milliliter. They grow rapidly at body temperature. They undoubtedly contribute to intestinal hygiene." *The Journal of Biological Chemistry* reports that eight ounces of yogurt has an antibiotic value equal to fourteen penicillin units. Medical observations have proved that the yogurt bacillus remains active even after passage through the intestines, indicating the bacilli were alive and working throughout the entire digestive system!

Man has searched endlessly for the Fountain of Youth and the Elixir of Life. They are not to be found in yogurt or any other single food. A healthy long life is a balance of nourishing natural foods, fresh air, cleanliness, moderate exercise and sufficient rest. You cannot neglect these needs and then expect a few cartons of yogurt to reclaim your health.

Many scientists and doctors recognize the medicinal worth of yogurt. Others, however, claim that experiments with it have not been completely scientifically controlled, thus they are not conclusive. Until more extensive, valid investigation is made, yogurt will remain a controversial food of fact and fiction.

# Yogurt By Any Other Name

Armenia . . . . . . . . . . . . . . . . . . . . . . . . . . mazun or matsoon

Balkans . . . . . . . . . . . . . . . . . . . . . . . . . . . . . . . . . tarho

Bulgaria . . . . . . . . . . . . . . . . . . . . . . . . . . . . . yogurt

Carpathian . . . . . . . . . . . . . . . . . . haslanka or urda

Chile . . . . . . . . . . . . . . . . . skuta or whey champagne

Finland . . . . . . . . . . . . . . . . . . . . . . . . . . . . plimae

France . . . . . . . . . . . . . . . . . . . . . . . . . . . yoghourt

Greece . . . . . . . . . . . . . . . . . . . . . . . . . . . . oxygala

Iceland . . . . . . . . . . . . . . . . . . . . . . . . . . . . . skyr

India . . . . . . . . . . . . . . . . . . . dahi, lassi, chass or matta

Iran . . . . . . . . . . . . . . . . . . . . . . . . . . . . . . . mast

Lapland . . . . . . . . . . . . . . . . . . . . . . . . . . . pauira

Norway . . . . . . . . . . . . . . . . . . . . . . . . kaelder milk

Russia . . . . . . . . . . . . . . . . . varenetz or prostokvasha

South Russia and Caucasus . . . . . . . . . . . . kefir or kuban

Sardinia . . . . . . . . . . . . . . . . . . . . . . . . . . . . gioddu

Siberia, South Russia
and Central Asia . . . . . . . . . . . . . . . . . . . . . . koumiss

Sicily . . . . . . . . . . . . . . . . . . . . . . . . . . . mezzoradu

Sweden . . . . . . . . . . . . . . . . . . . . . . . . . . . filmjolk

Turkestan . . . . . . . . . . . . . . . . . . . . . . . . . . . . busa

Turkey . . . . . . . . . . . . . . . . . . . . . . . . . . . . yogurt

17

# HOW YOGURT IS MADE COMMERCIALLY

An early 1970 Supermarket News survey indicated that sales of yogurt have increased 500% during the last decade. The addition of sweeteners, flavors and fruits was one reason for yogurt's skyrocketing sales. In 1968, Americans ate their way through 25 million dollars worth of this creamy product. In order to handle the growing demand, dairies have developed special processes and modern equipment to produce the finest quality yogurt in the most efficient, sanitary way possible. The processes, though seemingly complex, assure the consumer commercial brands as nutritious as the "home grown" variety.

## The Can-Set Method

*Blending the mix:* Precalculated amounts of pasteurized whole and skim milks are blended in a pasteurizer vat. As the mix is gently stirred, a predetermined amount of nonfat dry milk is shaken on the surface of the milk. The stirring is continued until the nonfat dry milk is dissolved.

*Homogenizing the mix:* The blended mix is heated in the pasteurizer vat to about 140º F. and then single-stage homogenized.

*Pasteurizing the mix:* The homogenized mix is returned to a pasteurizer vat and pasteurized at about 198º F. by the hold method. Then the mix is quickly cooled to about 110º F. in the same vat.

*Culturing the mix:* To the partially cooled mix the special culture is added while the milk is gently stirred. The stirring continues until the culture is thoroughly mixed with the milk mixture.

*Gelling the mix:* The cultured mix is drawn from the vat into 40-quart stainless steel cans and held at about 110º F. until the desired acidity for this stage is developed.

*Ripening the yogurt:* The gelled mix or yogurt is quickly cooled to about 40º F. and held undisturbed in the cans at this temperature until the final desired acidity has developed.

*Mixing the yogurt:* The solidly gelled mass is gently stirred in the cans until it resembles a light-bodied sour cream.

*Adding the fruit:* If a fruit-flavored yogurt is being made, a cooled, stabilized mixture of fruit pieces and sugar is gently folded into the plain yogurt in the cans.

*Packaging the yogurt:* The yogurt is gently turned into the hopper of the filling machine and is automatically pumped into the containers. As soon as the cups are filled, the packaging machine automatically applies the cup lids. During the packaging, a sample check is made every 15 minutes to determine the neatness of the package, application of the lid, the filled weight, accuracy of the code as well as the temperature of the yogurt. The approved, filled packages are then sent to the refrigerator and held there until loaded onto the delivery truck.

## The Container-Set Method

*Blending the mix:* Same as for the can-set.

*Homogenizing the mix:* Same as for the can-set method.

*Pasteurizing the mix:* Same as for the can-set method.

*Culturing the mix:* Same as for the can-set method.

*Adding the fruit:* If a fruit-flavored yogurt is being made, the fruit pieces, puree or juice are heated to the same temperature as the cultured mix, and then gently and thoroughly stirred in along with sugar.

*Packaging the mix:* The plain or flavored cultured mix is pumped through pipes leading to the filling machine. The cultured mix is automatically pumped into the cups and the packaging machine applies the lids to the cups.

*Gelling the mix:* The packaged yogurt is held at about 110° F. until the mix is gelled and the desired acidity for this stage has developed.

*Ripening the yogurt:* The filled containers are then stored at a temperature of about 40° F. for 36 hours before they are ready for shipment to consumers.

# HOW TO MAKE YOGURT AT HOME

Yogurt is very simple to make but like bread making, you have to get the feel for it. Getting the feel, however, does not take as long as making bread. Yogurt bacillus, like yeast, is very sensitive to temperature changes and the food it feeds upon. To insure the best possible results, be certain to use fresh milk and "starter" (commercial yogurt). Aged yogurt used as a starter is less dependable.

First find a suitable spot warm enough for the culture to grow. Yogurt culture should be kept at an even temperature, between 105° and 110°, from three to five hours. If the temperature rises above 120° the culture is killed. If the temperature drops below 95° the action slows. Yogurt making appliances may be purchased with temperature controls but they are not necessary. People have been making yogurt for 4,000 years without them.

Yogurt can be made in an oven by removing the appliance bulb and replacing it with a 100 watt bulb. Put a thermometer in the oven and leave it a few hours, checking occasionally to make sure the temperature stays between 105° and 110°. Because of variation in oven sizes, a different wattage bulb may be required. When the correct temperature is maintained, put yogurt milk mixture into a casserole dish, cover and set in a pan of warm water. Place the pan in the oven for the three to five hour incubation period. The yogurt mixture will maintain a more even temperature if kept in a pan of warm water.

## Basic Yogurt Recipe

*1 qt. milk, slim, skim or whole*
*2 T powdered milk*
*1 T yogurt, commercial*

Combine fresh milk and powdered milk in a heavy pan. Bring slowly to boiling point, stirring. Remove and transfer to a bowl to cool (about 110° or just above lukewarm). Blend a little milk with the yogurt until it is smooth, then add yogurt mixture to bowl of warm milk. Keep the cultured mixture covered and let set in a warm place. When mixture is the consistency of thick cream, refrigerate to chill before using.

Yogurt may also be made from pure lactic bacteria purchased from a health-food store. Follow the directions on the package or use the Basic Recipe. The first mixture with this bacteria requires a longer period of incubation than any subsequent batches. Save enough from each batch to make the next.

In the middle Eastern countries, yogurt is made every day. If you make yogurt every day, after a week or two your yogurt will become sweeter. It can be made tart if you use an aged yogurt as a starter. The desirable tartness depends entirely on your own personal taste. Some recipes, especially those for desserts, are best made with "sweet" yogurt. "Tangy" yogurt brings out the flavor of meats and some vegetables. If a tangier yogurt is desired, let the yogurt formula remain warm an hour or more after it has set. The acidity of yogurt depends on the length of time incubated and the culture used. More acid indicates more bacteria has grown.

Another very satisfactory method for incubating yogurt comes from the Balkan countries. Pour warm yogurt mixture into a covered casserole dish, wrap with a bit of old blanket for insulation, and put in a warm place. Leave it for twelve or more hours until the yogurt sets like thick cream. Make it at night and it will be ready the next day.

Small amounts of yogurt may be made in a wide mouth thermos. Pour the warm mixture in a thermos and cap it. Leave it until set, then remove the lid and place the thermos in refrigerator to chill. When chilled, spoon yogurt into a more suitable container. If you try to remove the yogurt before chilling, it will lose its solidity.

## Drained Yogurt

Put yogurt in a clean cloth bag and hang it on the kitchen faucet for an hour or two. Use drained yogurt in recipes for dips, spreads, sauces and dressing when a thicker consistency is desired.

## Yogurt Cream Cheese

Pour off surface whey and put yogurt in a bag made of three layers of cheese cloth. Hang the bag on the kitchen faucet and let drain into the sink overnight or until yogurt is the consistency of cream cheese. For a sharper cheese, use yogurt that is several days old.  Salt if desired. Cheese may be used, plain or mixed with minced chives, green onions, herbs or savory seeds to make delicious spreads and sandwich fillings. The cheese is excellent served with fresh papaya, peaches, avocado or melon.

## Soy Yogurt

Use ¼ cup yogurt to each quart liquid soy milk. Warm soy milk to 110° and add the yogurt culture. Keep in a warm spot until it reaches the desired thickness. When making a new batch, use a cup of this starter and make as before. Soy yogurt is higher in protein than yogurt made with cow's milk.

# Flavored Yogurt

For all variations, follow the same directions for incubating as in the Basic Yogurt Recipe.

## Caramel Yogurt

*6 T honey*
*3 T black strap molasses*
*1 qt. milk*
*1 T yogurt*

Mix honey and molasses into milk before heating.

## Prune Yogurt

*6 T pureed dried prunes, cooked*
  *honey to taste*
*1 qt. milk*
*1 T yogurt*

Scald milk and cool to lukewarm. Add other ingredients and mix thoroughly.

## Fresh Fruit Yogurt

*½ cup fresh fruit or berries*
*  honey to taste*
*1 qt. milk*
*1 T yogurt*

Scald milk and cool to lukewarm. Mix all ingredients.


## Carob Yogurt

*1 qt. milk*
*6 T carob powder*
*  honey to taste*
*1 T yogurt*

Blend carob and honey with milk; scald and cool to lukewarm. Add yogurt to warm mixture.

## Hints for Cooking with Yogurt

When cooking with yogurt, as with all high-protein, high-acid foods, spare the heat. Low temperatures and short heating periods are best. Whenever possible, stir in the yogurt shortly before removing the food from the heat, that is, just in time to let the food come to the serving temperature. Keep the temperature under 120° if you want to keep the bacillus active. If the yogurt must be added at the start of the cooking period, separation or curdling can be avoided by stirring into the yogurt a stabilizing mixture made of flour or cornstarch blended with a small amount of water.

- Fold, do not stir yogurt into other ingredients and it will keep a thick consistency.

- Yogurt may be substituted for buttermilk in many recipes. Thin yogurt to the consistency of buttermilk with a little water or milk.

- When yogurt is used in baking, use ½ teaspoon baking soda for each cup of yogurt used.

- Use yogurt as a sour cream substitute. Low fat yogurt has 138 calories per cup, whole milk yogurt has 165 calories and sour cream has 445 calories per cup. Yogurt gives a more tangy flavor to some dishes than sour cream. Another good calorie saver is to use yogurt as a partial substitute for mayonnaise. Use fifty percent mayonnaise and fifty percent yogurt.

- Stored at a refrigerator temperature of 35° to 45°, yogurt will keep in good condition for at least two weeks. The fresher it is when used, however, the better the flavor and consistency. Unopened containers with tightly fitted lids may be stored upside down to prevent air from entering the package; once opened, store the package upright. Yogurt becomes sharper with age.

- Making yogurt cheese is an excellent way to use aged yogurt.

# BLUE PRINT FOR YOGURT INCUBATING BOX

This easily constructed yogurt box is for those who want the convenience of constant temperature. Large amounts of yogurt can be made at one incubation. Test temperature by placing a thermometer inside and using a 60 watt light bulb. Temperature should remain around 105° to 110°.

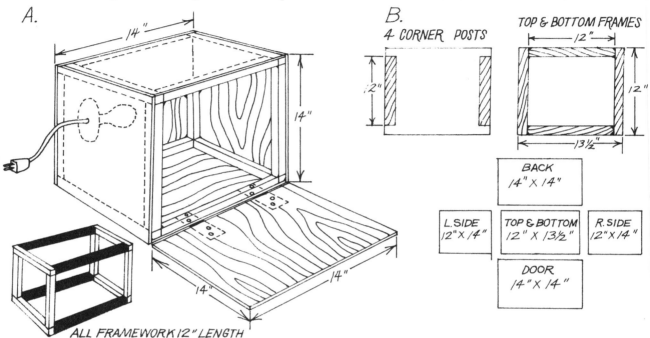

## Materials Required

1 sheet ¼" plywood 14" x 30". Cut into 2 pieces each 14" x 14" for door and back
1 sheet ¼" plywood 12" x 30". Cut into 4 pieces 2 sides 12" x 14"; top and bottom 12" x 13½"
12 12" lengths of 1" x 1" molding
2 hinges
1 latch set or hook-and-eye set
½ yard felt for lining
1 light fixture with cord and plug
   1" finishing nails
   white glue
   wood filler

## Construction Directions

Cut plywood as indicated. Spread glue on molding and nail in places shown in diagram "B". Fit molded plywood pieces together to form box as in diagram "A". Screw hinges and latch in place. Mount light fixture using bolt to secure. Counter-sink nails, then cover with wood filler. Glue lining to back, top and sides; use heavy foil to cover bottom for easy cleaning. Decorate outside with wallpaper, stain, paint, decoupage, or enhance by adding molding and carved wooden plaques.

# DIPS, SPREADS & SNACKS

## Tangy Tomato Dip

*½ cup yogurt*
*1 cup cottage cheese*
*¼ cup tomato juice*
*1 T onion flakes*
*¼ t dry mustard*
*1 t lemon juice*
*2 T catsup*
*1 t soy sauce*

Sieve cottage cheese and fold in yogurt. Blend in mustard, soy sauce, catsup, tomato juice, lemon juice and onion flakes. Makes 2 cups.

## Onion Dip

*1 cup yogurt*
*1 cup sour cream*
*1 envelope onion soup mix*

Blend thoroughly. Chill. Makes 2 cups.

## Hot Mustard Dip

*3 T dry mustard*
*2 T hot water*
*½ cup mayonnaise*
*2 T oil*
*¾ cup drained yogurt*

Mix together mustard and water. When smooth, mix mayonnaise, yogurt and oil until well blended. Fold in mustard; mix thoroughly. Makes 1½ cups.

## Roquefort Dip

*6 T coarsely crumbled Roquefort*
*   or bleu cheese*
*1 t onion salt*
*2 cups drained yogurt*

Mix well and chill. Makes 2 cups.

## Scandinavian Special

4 cans sardines, mashed
2 cups yogurt cream cheese
3 T lemon juice
½ cup minced parsley
2 T finely minced onions
1 t paprika
  salt and pepper

Mix sardines and yogurt cheese. Whip in other ingredients. After mixing well, spoon into lightly oiled mold. Refrigerate overnight or several hours to chill and blend flavors. Garnish with water cress or parsley springs. Serve with crackers.

## Tuna Dip

½ cup tuna
½ cup finely chopped cucumbers
2 t finely chopped chives
1 T lemon juice
1 cup yogurt

Mix all ingredients well and fold into the yogurt. Use salmon or caviar instead of tuna for variation. Makes 2 cups.

## Sherry Ham Dip

1 cup yogurt
½ cup ground cooked ham, well packed
2 t dry sherry
1 t prepared mustard
2 t minced onions

Mix all ingredients and chill until ready to serve. Makes 1½ cups.

## Clam Dip

1 cup clams, minced
½ cup cottage cheese
1½ cups yogurt
2 T minced onions
2 T lemon juice

Whirl all ingredients together in blender. Chill. Makes 2 cups.

## Chutney Dip

1 cup drained yogurt
¼ cup finely chopped chutney
¼ t ginger

Mix all ingredients and chill. Makes 1¼ cups.

## Meat Dip

½ cup yogurt cream cheese
¼ cup finely chopped cold meat
  or poultry
1 T chopped chives
2 T chopped pickles
6 green stuffed olives, finely chopped

Mix well and chill. May be used as a spread. Makes 1 cup.

## Paprika Dip

1 cup yogurt, drained
¼ cup mayonnaise
1 T chopped fresh basil
1 t paprika
½ t chili powder
  salt

Fold ingredients together and mix thoroughly. Makes 1¼ cups.

## Aegean Anchovy Dip

1 cup drained yogurt
2 t capers
1 t grated onion
2 t anchovy paste
  dash Worcestershire sauce
¼ cup mayonnaise

Blend all ingredients until smooth. Makes about 1¼ cups of dip.

## Anchovy Canape

toast strips or crackers
yogurt cream cheese
anchovy fillets
capers

Spread strips of toast or crackers generously with yogurt cream cheese. Place an anchovy fillet on each. Garnish with capers.

## Herb Dip

2 cups yogurt
1 t caraway seeds
2 t minced onion
2 t chopped green onion
½ t summer savory
  pinch thyme

Blend all ingredients and chill for several hours. Makes 2 cups.

## Polynesian Pineapple Spread

½ cup yogurt cream cheese
2 T crushed pineapple
½ cup finely chopped dates
½ cup shredded coconut

Mix well and chill. Spread on crackers or fill celery. Makes 2 cups.

## Mushroom Spread

1 lb. fresh mushrooms, finely chopped
1 large onion, finely chopped
4 T butter
  salt and pepper
1 cup yogurt

Saute mushrooms and onions in butter until golden brown. Let cool; add salt, pepper and yogurt. Mix well and chill. Serve with sesame wafers.

## El Bandido Spread

½ t chili powder
1 cup yogurt cream cheese
2 t finely chopped onion
¼ cup chopped pimiento, drained
¼ cup sliced olives
½ cup chopped sweet pickles

Mix all ingredients thoroughly. Makes 1¾ cups.

## Mediterranean Sandwich Spread

4 hard-cooked eggs, finely chopped
½ cup yogurt
¼ cup sliced black olives
4 green onions, finely chopped
1 clove garlic, finely chopped
1 T minced parsley
½ tomato, peeled and finely chopped

Mix together all ingredients. Use for sandwiches or spread on party crackers. Makes about 1½ cups.

## Yogurt Cheese Cakes

2 cups cottage cheese, drained
1½ cups yogurt, drained
2 T finely chopped chives
1 t caraway seed

Drain cottage cheese and yogurt overnight. Use a cotton cloth to drain yogurt and cheesecloth for cottage cheese. (Tying to faucet overnight is the easiest method). Remove yogurt and cottage cheese from cloth and add chives and caraway seed. Add salt and pepper if desired. Form into patties and place on lightly oiled cookie sheet. Bake at 275º until patties are dry and firm.

## Watercress Spread

½ cup finely chopped watercress
1 cup yogurt cream cheese
½ t grated onion
2 T mayonnaise
salt

Mix all ingredients well. Makes 1½ cups.

## Mexican Cheese Ball

1 lb. cheddar cheese
1 cup yogurt cream cheese
¼ cup minced ripe olives
2 4 oz. cans chopped green chilies
parsley

Combine all ingredients except parsley. Cream well and form in a large ball. Chill. Roll in minced parsley until completely coated. Serve with assorted crackers.

## Chinese Cheese Log

8 oz. cream cheese
2 cups yogurt cream cheese
1 cup drained pineapple
1 T curry powder
2 t soy sauce
¼ cup grated candied ginger
chopped salted almonds

Mix all ingredients except almonds. When completed blended, shape in to a log. Chill and then coat with chopped almonds.

## Bleu Cheese Balls

8 oz. bleu cheese
1½ cups yogurt cream cheese
¼ lb. butter
½ lb. hoope cheese
2 jiggers brandy
minced parsley, chives and tarragon

Mix all ingredients except herbs. When creamy, shape in walnut sized balls, then chill. Roll chilled balls in minced herbs. One large cheese ball may be made instead of small individual ones.

## Party Quiche

8 strips bacon, cooked and crumbled
1 onion, chopped
2 t margarine
1½ cup grated Swiss cheese
2 egg yolks
2 whole eggs
½ cup yogurt
½ t salt
  dash cayenne
1 9 inch unbaked pastry shell

Saute onion in margarine until transparent. With an electric beater, mix eggs, yogurt, salt and cayenne. Sprinkle cheese in bottom of pie shell; cover with crumbled bacon and onion. Pour egg mixture over bacon and onion, and bake in 375° oven for 35 to 40 minutes until custard is set. Cut in narrow pieshape wedges. Serve hot or cold. Quiche can be made ahead and frozen; defrost before baking.

## Lamb Temptations

1 lb. ground lamb
¼ cup yogurt
1 onion, minced
½ cup bread crumbs
1 green pepper, finely chopped
6 cloves garlic, minced
1 T Worcestershire sauce
2 t marjoram
1 t thyme
2 t salt
1 T curry powder
1 egg, beaten

Blend all ingredients except egg. Roll into ball of desired size, dip into beaten egg and saute on all sides until done.

## Green Devils

3 2½ oz. cans deviled ham
¼ cup coarsely crushed pretzels
½ t Worcestershire sauce
  pepper
1 cup yogurt cream cheese
  chopped chives

Blend deviled ham with pretzels, Worcestershire and pepper. Form into 25 balls, using a round half teaspoonful for each. Arrange on cookie sheet, then freeze for 30 minutes. Stir yogurt cream cheese until soft. Roll each firm ham ball in 1 tablespoon cream cheese or enough to cover, then in chopped chives. Refrigerate until served. Serve on picks. Makes 25.

## Blini

½ cup flour
½ cup milk
2 eggs, lightly beaten
  pinch baking soda
  pinch salt
2 oz. caviar
¾ cup yogurt
1 medium onion, finely chopped
  lemon wedges

In a bowl, mix flour, milk, eggs, baking soda and salt. Set aside for half an hour. Batter may be lumpy. Heat a dot of butter in a heavy skillet. When hot, pour batter a little at a time to form small pancakes. Cook for 1 minute on each side. Put cakes on a hot platter and cover with a towel until all cakes are cooked. Serve at once with about ½ teaspoon caviar, ½ teaspoon yogurt and a bit of chopped onion rolled in each pancake. Serve lemon wedges on the side. Makes about 2 dozen.

## Chicken Piroshki

*2 cups sifted flour*
*½ t salt*
*½ cup soft butter*
*½ cup yogurt*
*1 cup cooked chicken, veal or*
  *chicken livers, minced*
*1 3 oz. can chopped mushrooms, drained*
*1 T butter*
*1 hard-cooked egg, minced*
*½ cup yogurt*
  *dash of each, garlic salt,*
  *cayenne, paprika and dill weed*

To make pastry, sift flour and salt; blend in ½ cup butter. Work in ½ cup yogurt. Wrap in waxed paper and chill overnight. To make filling, saute meat and mushrooms in 1 tablespoon butter for 2 or 3 minutes. Add egg, garlic salt, cayenne, paprika and dill. Remove from heat and add yogurt; mix well. Roll out pastry to ¼ inch thickness. Cut out with floured 3½ inch cutter. Put 1 tablespoon filling on one side of each round; wet edges and fold over. Pinch edges to seal. Put on greased cookie sheet and bake in 375º oven about 15 minutes. Serve hot as an appetizer, with soup or as a snack. Makes 16.

## Deviled Eggs

*6 eggs, hard-cooked*
*3 T yogurt cream cheese, whipped*
*2 T mayonnaise*
*1 t chopped chives*
*3 minced anchovies*
  *nutmeg*

Cut eggs in half lengthwise. In bowl, mix egg yolks, mayonnaise, yogurt cheese, chives and anchovies. When thoroughly mixed, fill egg halves with mixture and dust with nutmeg.

## Yogurt Cheese Balls

Form yogurt cheese into 1 inch balls. Put the balls on a cloth to dry for 10 or 12 hours. Place dried cheese balls in a jar and cover with olive oil. Yogurt cheese balls will keep this way several weeks, even unrefrigerated. For variation, add crushed clove of garlic to the oil. Makes an excellent appetizer.

# Raw Vegetables

Add color and variety to your dips and spreads. Select an assortment of fresh raw vegetables, arrange on a tray and serve crisp and cold.

Asparagus, *young and tender*
Beets, *cut into wedges, slices or fingers*
Bell Pepper, *sticks, wedges or rings*
Broccoli Buds, *bite size*
Broccoli Stalks, *peeled and cut into sticks or slices*
Brussels Sprouts, *small and young*
Carrot Sticks
Cauliflower Flowerets
Celery Stalks
Chard Stalks
Egg Plant, *unpeeled, cut into sticks and dipped in lemon juice.*
Kohlarbi, *peeled and sliced or cut into fingers*
Mushrooms, *whole or sliced*
Sweet Red Pepper, *cut into wedges or rings*
Potatoes, *white or sweet, thin slices or sticks*
Radishes, *red and white*
Summer Squash, *cut in wedges*
Turnips, *cut in slices or sticks*
Cherry Tomatoes
Yellow Tomatoes
Zucchini, *cut into rings or sticks*

# SOUPS

## Squash Soup

1 cup yogurt
4 cups milk
½ bay leaf
3 T flour
2 cups summer squash,
  cooked and mashed
1 cup diced celery, par-boiled
3 T butter
  salt

In a saucepan, mix yogurt, milk, bay leaf, chives and heat to boiling point. Cover, remove from heat and set aside. In another saucepan, mix flour and butter, add squash, celery and salt. Simmer a few minutes over low heat, then combine the two mixtures. Remove the bay leaf; serve hot and garnished with chopped chives. Serves 6 to 8.

## Belgian Watercress Soup

4 medium potatoes
2 cups potato water
3 T butter
2 medium onions, chopped
2 bunches watercress, chopped
1 cup milk
¾ cup yogurt
  salt and pepper
  whole-wheat croutons

Scrub potatoes and cook with jackets until done. Save the water. Peel and dice potatoes. In a large saucepan, saute onions in butter for 3 or 4 minutes. Add potatoes, potato water, watercress and seasonings. Simmer covered for 5 minutes. Add milk and yogurt to the mixture; heat but do not boil. Garnish with croutons. Serves 6.

## Spinach Soup Tanya

2 bunches spinach, finely chopped
½ lb. lamb, cut in small pieces
2 or 3 cloves garlic
1 onion, chopped
1½ cups yogurt
3 cups water

In a large saucepan, saute onion until transparent. Add garlic and lamb; brown lightly, and add water. Cover and cook over low heat until meat is tender. Add spinach and cook 5 minutes. Stir in yogurt and reheat. Serves 4.

## Spinach Cider Soup

4 cups meat stock
2 carrots, diced
1 stalk celery, chopped
3 T butter
4 T flour
1 onion, chopped
½ clove garlic, crushed
½ lb. spinach, chopped
1 T minced parsley
1 t dill
½ cup apple cider
1 cup yogurt
4 egg yolks
  salt and pepper

Bring stock to boil in large saucepan, add carrots and celery; cook until tender. Remove from heat. In a small skillet, melt butter and saute onion until transparent. Add garlic and flour; cook for 2 minutes. Combine half a cup of soup stock with onion mixture, stirring constantly; add mixture to cooked vegetables. Add spinach, parsley, dill and cider. Season and bring to a boil. Beat yogurt and egg yolks; pour into soup. Reheat, but do not allow to boil. Serve hot. Serves 6.

## Mrs. Chaudhuri's Chowder

½ lb. mushrooms, coarsley chopped
1 medium onion, chopped
2 T margarine
1 cup diced raw potatoes
1 cup boiling water
2 egg yolks, beaten
¼ cup cooking sherry
2 cups yogurt
¼ t thyme leaves
¼ t mace
¼ t cloves
  salt and pepper
  chopped parsley

In a large saucepan, saute mushrooms and onions in margarine for 3 or 4 minutes. Add potatoes and water; bring to a boil and cook for 10 minutes or until potatoes are tender. Add milk, egg yolks, sherry, yogurt, thyme, cloves, mace and seasonings. Heat just to boiling point. Garnish with parsley. Serves 6.

## Avocado Soup

½ dried chili pepper, crushed
3 large avocados
3 cups chicken stock
1 cup yogurt
1 t salt
  dash cayenne pepper

In a blender, whirl at low speed 2 chopped avocados, chili pepper and chicken stock. When smooth, pour in top ot double boiler. Heat to boiling point over direct heat, then set pan back on bottom part and continue cooking over boiling water. Add yogurt; mix well and heat again to a slow simmer. Cut the remaining avocado in cubes. Just before serving, add seasoning and avocado cubes. Serves 4.

## Mushroom Soup

1 lb. fresh mushrooms, thinly sliced
2 cups milk
¼ cup powdered skim milk
2 shallots, minced
2 T oil
1 cup yogurt
4 egg yolks, beaten
½ cup sweet sherry
  salt

Dissolve powdered milk in fresh milk and add mushrooms to marinate. In a deep saucepan, saute shallots in oil for 5 minutes; add mushroom mixture, yogurt, salt and pepper. Simmer over low heat for 25 minutes. Stir occasionally. Just before serving, add egg yolks and sherry. Mix well. Serves 4.

## Creamy Potato Soup

3 cups diced raw potatoes
2 cups water
1 bouillon cube
2 cups milk
¼ cup chopped onions
1 cup chopped celery
2 T margarine
1 T flour
½ cup yogurt
  salt and pepper
  minced parsley

Cook potatoes, celery and onions in water, simmering until tender. Liquefy in a blender. Dissolve bouillon cube in a little boiling water and add milk, bouillon and margarine to the blended vegetables. Mix yogurt with flour until smooth; add to soup and bring to a slow boil. Simmer over low heat until thickened, stirring constantly. Add salt and pepper to taste. Garnish with minced parsley. Serves 6.

## Arabian Night Soup

1 cup dried peas
1 cup meat stock or bouillon
3 cups water
1 chopped onion
3 T oil
1 cup yogurt
1 t chopped parsley
  salt and pepper

Soak peas overnight. Simmer slowly in water and meat stock with onion until cooked. Add oil, salt and pepper. Simmer for 15 to 20 minutes, stirring occasionally. When ready to serve, add yogurt, stirring until well blended. Reheat and serve garnished with chopped parsley. Serves 4.

## Balkan Barley Soup

3 T pearl barley
1 qt. clear stock
1 t salt
¼ t pepper
2 cups yogurt
½ cup sour cream
1 egg
4 T melted butter
2 T finely chopped parsley

Soak barley overnight in enough water to cover. Drain and put into a large saucepan with stock, salt and pepper. Cook over low heat for 2 hours or until barley is soft. In a bowl, beat yogurt, sour cream and egg. Gradually add 1 cup of soup to yogurt mixture, stirring vigorously. Then pour yogurt mixture in soup. Add butter and parsley and stir well. Heat soup to just below boiling point. Serves 4 to 6.

## Cranberry Borscht

½ cup cranberries
4 cups water
1 medium onion, sliced
1 cup canned julienne beets
½ cup beet liquor
1 cup chopped cabbage
1 T brown sugar
  salt
¾ cup yogurt
2 hard cooked eggs, chopped

Simmer cranberries until skins are popped, then strain. To cranberries, add onion and cabbage. Cook until tender. Add shredded beets, salt, sugar, yogurt and beet liquor. Chill. Garnish with chopped egg. Serves 6.

## Hungarian Beef Soup

3 T oil
2 onions, chopped
4 small potatoes, diced
4 carrots, sliced
2 stalks celery, chopped
2 small turnips, diced
3 small tomatoes, quartered
1 t paprika
½ t caraway seed
2 cups hot water
2 cups diced cooked beef
1 cup yogurt
  salt to taste

Heat oil in large, heavy sauce pan. Add chopped onions and cook until lightly browned. Add potatoes, carrots, celery, turnips and tomatoes. Sprinkle with paprika and caraway seed. Mix well and add hot water. Cover tightly and simmer vegetables until tender. Salt to taste. Add meat and yogurt, stirring until well heated. Serves 6.

## Blender Beet Borscht

1 qt. stock
1 cup beet juice
1 cup beets, cooked and cubed
  juice and rind of 1 lemon
1 cup yogurt
½ t salt
1 sprig of parsley
½ t tarragon

Combine all ingredients in a blender and whirl until smooth. Chill 3 or 4 hours. Serve garnished with minced chives. Serves 6.

## Chicken Soup

1 broiler chicken
6 cups water
1 carrot, diced
1 onion, chopped
1 stalk celery, diced
1 cup yogurt
2 egg yolks
3 whole eggs
1 t fennel
1 t marjoram
  salt and pepper

Put chicken in large saucepan. Add water and bring to boil slowly, removing the scum as it rises. Cook chicken 2½ hours or until tender. Remove chicken and add vegetables; cook until tender. Cut chicken in thin strips, julienne fashion. Return pieces of chicken to saucepan. Beat yogurt in a bowl with egg yolks; add the whole eggs and beat until smooth. Thin egg mixture with a little of the stock and season with salt and pepper. Add egg mixture to soup and stir well. Reheat to boiling point. Serve hot, garnished with fennel and marjoram. Serves 6.

## Hearty Meat Ball Soup

½ lb. ground beef
1 small onion, finely chopped
½ t salt
¼ t pepper
4 cups yogurt
¼ cup rice
1 egg
1 T flour
1½ t salt
½ t pepper
4 cups water
½ cup chopped parsley
½ cup chopped green onions
½ cup canned garbonzo beans
1 t dill

In a bowl, mix meat, onion and seasonings; shape into balls the size of walnuts. In a 3 quart pot, put yogurt, rice, egg, flour and seasonings. Mix well. Add water and cook over very low heat, stirring constantly for about 20 minutes or until mixture thickens. Add meat balls to yogurt mixture and let simmer for 10 minutes. Add parsley, green onions, garbonzo beans and dill. Simmer for another 10 minutes, stirring often to prevent sticking. Garnish with garlic butter. Serves 8.

## Garlic Butter

Chop one or two cloves of garlic and saute in 3 tablespoons butter, add 1 tablespoon dried powdered mint. Serve a teaspoon of hot sauce on each serving of soup.

## Yogurt Noodle Soup

1 egg, beaten
3 cups yogurt
1 cup egg noodles, broken
2 cups water
1 t salt
1 T butter
2 t dry mint, crushed
1 small onion, chopped

Mix yogurt, egg and salt. Beat for 3 minutes and add water. Bring to a boil over high heat, stirring constantly. Add noodles and cook slowly until tender. Saute onions in butter, add mint and pour into soup. Simmer for 5 minutes. Serves 6.

## Oatmeal Soup

2 cups water
2 cups yogurt
½ cup oatmeal
2 t salt
2 T butter
1 t chopped mint leaves
1 small onion, chopped

Cook oatmeal in salted water for 5 minutes. Put yogurt in large bowl and pour oatmeal mixture gradually into the yogurt to prevent curdling. Pour mixture back into pan; put on low heat to keep warm. Melt butter and saute onions; add chopped mint leaves and pour over soup. Serves 4.

## Caribbean Nut Soup

*½ lb. almond or cashew nuts, finely ground*
*3 T rice flour*
*3 T butter*
*2 cups milk*
*1 cup yogurt*
*1 t salt*

Mix all ingredients and simmer gently until creamy. Serves 4.

## Classic Turkish Yogurt Soup

*2 cups yogurt*
*3 cucumbers, chopped*
*1 t dill*
*1 small clove garlic*
*3 T oil*
*1 t dill seeds*
*1 T mint leaves*
*1 lemon*

Grate rind of lemon, then cut and juice both halves. Mix all ingredients in blender until smooth. Chill for 2 or 3 hours. Serves 4 to 6.

## Summer Soup

*2 cups yogurt*
*1 can split pea soup*
*¼ t salt*
*  pepper*
*  chives*

Combine soup, salt, pepper and mix well. Bring just to a boil, then cool. When cool, add yogurt and mix well. Serve chilled and garnished with chopped chives. Serves 4.

## Calcutta Soup

*1 boiled egg, chopped*
*½ cup raisins*
*1 cup cold water*
*3 cups yogurt*
*½ cup light cream*
*6 ice cubes*
*1 cucumber, chopped*
*¼ cup chopped green onions*
*  salt and pepper*
*1 T parsley, chopped*
*1 T fresh dill, chopped*
*  or 1 t dill weed*

Soak raisins in the cold water for 5 minutes. Put yogurt in large mixing bowl; add cream, egg, ice cubes, cucumbers, green onions, salt and pepper. Add raisins and water to yogurt mixture. Mix well and refrigerate for 2 or 3 hours. Serve garnished with parsley and dill. Serves 6.

## Frosty Cucumber Soup

*2 cups buttermilk*
*2 cups yogurt*
*1½ cups finely chopped cucumbers*
*1 T finely chopped green onion*
*1 T chopped fresh dill*
*  or 1 t dill weed*
*2 t lemon juice*
*2 t salt*
*  pepper*
*6 thin lemon slices*

Blend together buttermilk and yogurt. Combine mixture with cucumbers, onion, salt, pepper, dill and lemon juice. Chill. Just before serving, mix again and pour into chilled consomme cups. Garnish with lemon slices. Serves 6.

## Vichysoisse

3 T oil
3 leeks, chopped
1 onion, chopped
3 potatoes, cubed
1 qt. chicken stock
1 t salt
2 cups milk
1 cup yogurt
¼ cup chives, minced

Heat oil in saucepan; saute leeks and onions. Add potatoes, stock and salt. Cover and simmer for 30 minutes. Puree mixture. Return to saucepan and add milk. Cover and heat just until soup comes to a boil. Remove from heat and chill. Blend in yogurt and garnish with chives. Serves 6 to 8.

## Cherry Danish Soup

2 lbs. ripe cherries, pitted
2 cups water
1 2 inch cinnamon stick
2 cloves
¼ t salt
2 cups Burgundy, claret or rose wine
1 T cognac or cherry brandy
  honey
½ cup yogurt

In a saucepan, slowly cook cinnamon, cloves, salt and cherries in water. When cherries are tender, rub through a sieve; add wine, brandy and honey to taste. Reheat slowly, do not boil. When steaming hot, remove from heat. Let cool and refrigerate to chill thoroughly. Just before serving, swirl in yogurt. Makes 4 servings.

## Fresh Garden Soup

1 cup finely chopped onions
1 cup diced unpeeled cucumber
½ sweet red pepper, finely chopped
1 large tomato, chopped
½ cup chopped watercress
3 cups yogurt
  salt and pepper
  watercress

Combine all vegetables and refrigerate until well chilled. Fold vegetables into yogurt, add salt and pepper. Blend gently. Serve in chilled soup bowls and garnish with sprig of watercress. Serves 4.

## Tomato Soup

2 large cans tomatoes
5 green onions, minced
1 t salt
1 t sugar
¼ t marjoram
¼ t thyme leaves
1 t curry powder
2 t grated lemon rind
  juice 1 lemon
1 cup yogurt
  pepper

Force tomatoes with juice through coarse sieve. Add remaining ingredients, except yogurt. Mix well and chill several hours. Strain again through sieve. Beat in yogurt with rotary beater. Serve very cold in bouillon cups with garnish of chopped parsley. Serves 6.

# SALADS

### Cool Tropical Salad

*1 small fresh pineapple*
*1 cup mango chunks or melon balls*
*1 cup diced papaya or fresh peaches*
*2 cups yogurt*
*2 T honey*
*1 cup sliced strawberries*
*4 sprigs fresh mint*

Cut pineapple in quarters, length-wise. Remove core; slice pineapple from shell and cut in cubes. Refrigerate empty shell to chill until serving time. Toss 1 cup of cubed pineapple with mango and papaya. Chill. To serve, put 1/3 cup yogurt on each pineapple shell and cover with mixed fruit. Top with layer of remaining yogurt, which has been sweetened with honey and cover with sliced strawberries. Garnish each serving with whole strawberry and a sprig of fresh mint. Makes 4 generous servings.

### Red Orange Salad

*2 cups Julienne beets, drained*
*1/8 t salt*
*1 t grated lemon rind*
*1 T lemon juice*
*1 T orange juice*
*2 cups yogurt*
*6 orange sections*
　*watercress*
　*lettuce or choice of mixed salad*
　*greens*

Combine beets, salt, lemon juice and lemon rind. Chill for several hours. Drain beets. Fold grated orange rind and orange juice into yogurt. Arrange salad greens on individual plates. For each salad, serve 1/3 cup of beet mixture topped with 1/3 cup yogurt mixture. Garnish with orange sections and watercress leaves. Serves 6.

## Big Apple Salad

3 big apples, finely chopped
2 T honey
1 T lemon juice
½ cup chopped dates or raisins
½ cup chopped nuts
1 cup yogurt
½ cup shredded coconut
    salad greens

Mix honey, lemon juice, dates or raisins and chopped nuts. Fold in apples and yogurt. Spoon on greens for individual servings. Garnish each serving with shredded coconut. Serves 4.

## Magnificent Mandarin Salad

1 cup yogurt
1 T honey
2 carrots, grated
2 large apples, chopped
2 stalks celery, finely chopped
1 small can mandarin oranges, drained
1 t grated orange peel
    salt and pepper
    watercress or lettuce

In a bowl, mix yogurt, honey and orange peel. Fold in vegetables and fruit. Season and serve on a bed of watercress. Serves 4 to 6.

## California Fruit Salad

1½ cups yogurt
2 T orange marmalade
1 large grapefruit, sectioned
1 large orange, sectioned
1 avocado, sliced lengthwise
    romaine or other greens
    seedless white grapes

Wash grapes and chill. Whip together orange marmalade and yogurt. Arrange slices of avocado with sections of orange and grapefruit on romaine. Top with yogurt mixture, garnish with chilled grapes. Serves 6.

## Banana Split Salad

1 cup yogurt
½ cup crushed pineapple, drained
1 T honey
4 bananas, peeled
¼ cup chopped nuts
½ cup crushed strawberries

Mix yogurt, pineapple and honey. Cut bananas in half, lengthwise. For each serving, use 2 banana halves. Put ¼ cup yogurt mixture on each serving. Sprinkle with chopped nuts and top with crushed berries. Red raspberries may be substituted for strawberries. Serves 4.

## Jewish Squash Salad

*8 small summer squash, thinly sliced*
*2 T fresh mint or dill*
*1 cup yogurt*
*¼ cup sour cream*
*¼ cup mayonnaise*

Put squash in saucepan and add just enough water to half cover the vegetable. Bring to a boil and remove from heat. Squash should be crisp. Drain and chill thoroughly. Gently mix in the herbs, seasoning, and garlic if used. Whip yogurt, mayonnaise and sour cream until smooth. Pour mixture over squash. Serves 4.

## Potato Supper Salad

*5 cups sliced cooked potatoes*
*½ cup diced celery*
*¼ cup chopped green onions with tops*
*½ cup thinly sliced radishes*
*¼ cup chopped green pepper*
*2 t salt*
  *pepper*
*¼ cup French dressing*
*1½ cup yogurt*
*8 thin slices ham*
*2 hard-cooked eggs, quartered*
  *salad greens*

Mix potatoes, celery, green onions, radishes and green pepper. Sprinkle with salt and pepper. Lightly mix in French dressing and chill 2 or 3 hours. Just before serving, fold in yogurt. Place greens on serving platter and top with potato mixture. Arrange rolls of ham around salad. Garnish with eggs. Serves 8.

## Spanish Onion and Cucumber Salad

*1 cup yogurt*
*2 T lemon juice*
*½ t black pepper*
*¼ t dill weed*
*1 t chopped parsley*
  *salt*
*1 large spanish onion, sliced*
*2 unpeeled cucumbers, sliced*
  *fresh spinach leaves*

In a bowl, mix yogurt, lemon juice, pepper, dill, parsley and salt. Line salad bowl with young leaves of spinach. Pleace on a layer of cucumber, then a layer of onion rings and then some dressing. Repeat the layers, topping with the dressing. Refrigerate for 1 or 2 hours. Serve with pumpernickel or very dark rye bread. Serves 4.

## Tossed Green Salad

*3 small heads romaine*
  *pinch sugar*
*3 T olive oil*
  *salt and pepper*
*1 cup yogurt*

Thoroughly wash lettuce; remove the outer brused leaves and tear the remainder in pieces. (Before putting the leaves into the bowl they should be dried. If a lettuce drier is not available, put the leaves into a towel and gently turn the leaves over and over until they are dry.) Mix salt, pepper, sugar and oil with yogurt. Pour sauce over lettuce and gently toss the leaves over and over until evenly coated with dressing. Serves 6.

## Spinach Salad

1 lb. fresh spinach, washed
  and dried
½ t salt
  dash pepper
2 hard cooked eggs, chopped
1 cup yogurt
4 slices bacon, fried crisp
  lettuce or other greens

Chill spinach and chop coarsley. Add salt, pepper and egg to ¼ cup yogurt. Just before serving, fold in spinach. Serve on lettuce, topping with remaining yogurt. Garnish with crumbled bacon. Makes 4 servings.

## Russian Style Cucumbers

2 egg yolks
¼ t salt
¼ t dry mustard
¼ t paprika
1 cup yogurt
1 T lemon juice
2 unpeeled cucumbers, thinly sliced
  chopped parsley

To make the dressing, combine egg yolk, salt, mustard and paprika in a bowl. Beat with fork until fluffy. Gradually beat in yogurt and lemon juice. Chill. When ready to serve, arrange cucumbers and dressing in alternate layers. Top with layer of dressing. Sprinkle with parsley. Serves 4.

## Slavic Salad

4 hard boiled eggs, chopped
3 pickled gherkins, chopped
2 cups cold potatoes, diced
1 large beetroot, cooked and diced
¾ cup yogurt
4 T olive oil
1 T wine vinegar
2 oz. black olives, pitted
¼ lb. chopped mixed nuts
  salt and pepper

Combine all ingredients and toss lightly until well mixed. Chill before serving. Serves 4.

## Stuffed Tomatoes

1 large cucumber
2 cups yogurt
1 cup finely chopped chipped beef
1 T finely chopped onion
¼ cup finely chopped celery
6 medium tomatoes
  salt
  salad greens
1 green pepper, stems and seeds removed

Chop enough cucumber to make ¼ cup; slice remainder for garnish. Mix yogurt with chopped cucumber, onion, celery, chopped beef and salt. Remove stems and ends from washed, chilled tomatoes. Cut each tomato in 6 wedges halfway down and spread open slightly. Fill with yogurt mixture. Serve on lettuce leaf. Garnish with sliced cucumber and green pepper rings. Serve with warm Jewish corn rye bread and butter. Makes a tasty luncheon for 6.

## Neptune Salad

1 lb. cooked shrimp, shelled and deveined
4 cups shelled peas, cooked and chilled
1 cup yogurt
½ cup mayonnaise
1 T lemon juice
½ t salt
½ t dill weed
4 hard-cooked eggs, chopped
½ cup chopped sweet pickle
2 T chopped green onion
1 cup thinly sliced celery
   lettuce

Chill shrimp. Cook peas until barely tender. Pour into colander and cool under cold running water. Chill. Combine yogurt, mayonnaise, lemon juice, salt and dill weed; refrigerate. Just before serving combine all ingredients. Serve in lettuce cups. Makes 6 servings.

## Shrimp Stuffed Avocados

¾ t dill weed
½ t seasoned salt
¼ cup yogurt
1 cup chopped cooked shrimp
½ cup chopped unpeeled cucumber
¼ cup grated carrots
¼ cup chopped celery
2 T sliced green onions
3 avocados, halved
   lemon juice

In a small bowl, combine dill weed and seasoned salt; stir in yogurt. Cover and chill. In a bowl combine shrimp, cucumber, carrots, celery and green onions. Add yogurt dressing and toss lightly. Dip cut surface of avocado halves in lemon juice. Spoon salad into avocado halves. Arrange on platter to serve 6.

## Hot Potato Salad

4 cups hot cooked cubed potatoes
¼ cup chopped green onion with tops
1 cup yogurt
2 T prepared mustard
1 t salt
1 t sugar

Combine potatoes and onion. Heat yogurt, but do not boil. Blend in seasonings. Pour over potatoes and onion; toss lightly to coat potatoes. Serve topped with smoked sausage links, frankfurters or ham slices. Makes 6 servings.

## Caraway Cabbage Slaw

5 T mayonnaise
¼ t dry mustard
1 T vinegar
1 T honey
½ t salt
   dash pepper
1 pimiento, chopped
1½ T finely chopped green pepper
2 T grated onion
½ cup seedless grapes, cut in half
1 t caraway seed
1½ cups yogurt
4 cups shredded cabbage

Mix mustard, mayonnaise, vinegar, honey, salt and pepper. Add pimiento, green pepper, onion, grapes and caraway seed. Mix well. Fold in yogurt and add cabbage. Toss lightly to mix. Serves 6.

## Lobster Salad Bowl

*1/3 cup chili sauce*
*1 T finely chopped onion*
*2 t vinegar*
*2 t lemon juice*
*½ t salt*
*1½ cups yogurt*
*1 small head lettuce, torn*
*6 oz. Swiss cheese, cut in strips*
*2 cups cooked lobster, chopped*
*½ cup chopped parsley*
*2 T sliced green onions*
*2 hard-cooked eggs, sliced*
*2 tomatoes, cut in wedges*

In a small bowl, combine chili sauce, chopped onion, vinegar, lemon juice and salt. Fold in yogurt. Chill. In a salad bowl, toss together lettuce, cheese, lobster, parsley and green onions. Garnish with egg slices and tomato wedges. Serve dressing separately. Serves 6.

## Avocado Salad Mold

*1 envelope unflavored gelatin*
*½ cup water*
*2 T honey*
*1 cup yogurt*
*1 medium avocado*
*2 T lemon juice*

Sprinkle gelatin over water in saucepan. Over low heat stir until gelatin dissolves, about 2 or 3 minutes. Remove from heat; stir in sugar until dissolved. In a bowl beat avocado meat until creamy; add yogurt, gelatin and lemon juice. Pour into 2-cup mold or 4 individual molds. Chill until set. Serve plain on lettuce leaf or garnish with fruit. Serves 6.

## Roquefort Mold

*¼ lb. Roquefort cheese*
*1 envelope unflavored gelatin*
*½ cup yogurt*
*1 T finely chopped onion*
*1 T lemon juice*
  *paprika*
*2½ cups chopped celery*
*½ cup water*

Sprinkle gelatin over water in saucepan. Stir over low heat until gelatin dissolves, about 2 or 3 minutes. Remove from heat, add lemon juice, paprika and onion. In bowl, cream Roquefort and cream cheese. Add gelatin mixture, celery and yogurt to creamed Roquefort mixture. Refrigerate. When mixture begins to thicken, add celery. Serves 4.

## Regal Plum Mold

*2 envelopes unflavored gelatin*
*1 cup cold water*
*1 30 oz. can purple plums*
*3 T lime juice*
*½ t salt*
*1 cup dry cottage cheese*
*1 cup diced celery*
*1 cup yogurt*
  *salad greens*
  *paprika*

Soften gelatin in cold water. Drain plums. To plum juice, add lime juice and enough water to make 1½ cups liquid. Heat and add to gelatin with salt. Chill until syrupy. To pitted and diced plums, add cottage cheese, celery and yogurt; mix with gelatin. Pour into mold; chill until firm. Unmold on greens and garnish with yogurt, topped with paprika. Serves 6 to 8.

## Cucumber Chiller

1 envelope gelatin
¼ cup cold water
2 T lime juice
2 drops green coloring
1 cup crushed pineapple, drained
½ unpeeled cucumber, thinly sliced
2 T honey
  dash salt
  dash Tabasco
1 cup diced peeled cucumber
1 cup yogurt
  watercress

Soften gelatin in cold water. Combine lime juice and green coloring with juice from pineapple. Add boiling water to make 1 cup liquid and add to gelatin. Chill until syrupy. Grease mold, place a few cucumber slices in mold with a little gelatin. Chill until firm. Add pineapple, seasonings and diced cucumbers to remaining gelatin; fold in yogurt and pour into mold. Chill until firm. Unmold on watercress with remaining cucumber slices for garnish. Serves 6 to 8.

## Soybean-Cheese Salad

2 cups cooked soybeans, drained
½ cup grated cheese
1 cup chopped celery
1 cup cooked, diced carrots
½ cup diced cucumber
½ cup yogurt
  salt and pepper
  watercress
2 tomatoes, sliced

Mix together soybeans, cheese, celery, carrots, cucumber and a small amount of watercress. Fold in yogurt, salt and pepper. Place in lettuce-lined salad dish; decorate with slices of tomatoes and sprigs of watercress. Serves 4 to 6.

# SAUCES & DRESSINGS

### Fresh Mint Dressing

*¼ cup finely chopped mint*
*1 T honey*
*2 t lemon juice*
*pinch salt*
*2 cups yogurt*

Mix mint and honey; let stand 5 to 10 minutes. Fold mint, lemon juice and salt into yogurt. Chill. Excellent with fruit salads. Makes 2 cups.

### Walnut-Ginger Dressing

Mix ¼ cup finely chopped candied ginger, ½ cup minced walnuts and 1 tablespoon honey. Fold in 2 cups yogurt. Ideal on fruit salads. Makes 2½ cups.

### Golden Goddess Topping

Mix yogurt with honey to taste. This is delicious on strawberries, raspberries, seedless grapes, peaches or any sliced fruit.

### Boysenberry Sauce

Stir 2 tablespoons honey into 1 cup boysenberry yogurt. Try this on Sunday Brunch Pancakes.

### Marmalade Sauce Pershing

Whip 1 to 3 tablespoons marmalade with a cup yogurt. Excellent with fruit.

## Low Calorie Dressing

*1 cup yogurt*
*½ t dry mustard*
*1 t salt*
*1 to 2 t paprika*
*2 T finely chopped onion*

Mix well and refrigerate 1 hour before serving.

Variations: Add 1 teaspoon of any of the following: minced fresh basil, marjoram, savory or dill. Makes 1 cup.

## Tarragon Dressing

*1 cup yogurt*
*2 t chopped parsley*
*½ t dill weed*
*2 T tarragon vinegar*
*1 T olive oil*
*½ t salt*
  *dash pepper*
  *dash garlic powder*

Blend all ingredients. Chill. Makes 1½ cups of dressing for cooked vegetables or coleslaw.

## Cheddar Cheese Dressing

*1 cup yogurt*
*1 cup grated cheddar cheese*
*2 T vinegar*
*1 t caraway seed*

Combine all ingredients, chill. Makes 2½ cups. Serve on green salads or sliced tomatoes.

## Egg Dressing

*1 cup yogurt*
*2 egg yolks, well beaten*
*½ t dry mustard*
*1 T honey*
  *pinch paprika*
  *pinch cayenne*
*1 T vinegar*
  *salt*

Combine all ingredients and mix thoroughly. Makes 1½ cups.

## Thousand Island Dressing

*1 cup Egg Dressing*
*1 hard-cooked egg, chopped*
*2 T chili sauce*
*1 t pimiento, chopped*
*1 T onion, finely minced*
*1 T green pepper, finely minced*

Fold all ingredients into egg dressing, mixing well. Makes 1½ cups.

## Orange Dressing

*½ cup orange juice*
  *dash salt*
*4 T honey*
*2 egg yolks, beaten*
*1 cup yogurt*
  *pinch of cinnamon*

Blend orange juice, salt and honey in top of double boiler. Cook over hot water. Gradually add egg yolks, stirring constantly. Continue cooking and stirring until slightly thickened. Remove from heat; cool. Fold in yogurt and cinnamon. Makes 1¾ cups.

## Chestnut Sauce

1½ lbs. chestnuts
1 cup yogurt
2 T white wine
1 T butter

Boil chestnuts until soft, remove skins. Put through a fine grinder. Blend together yogurt, wine and butter. Add ground chestnuts and mix well. Cook 3 minutes over low heat, stirring constantly. Makes about 2½ cups.

## Chili Con Queso Sauce

1 cup grated Monterey Jack cheese
½ cup yogurt
½ cup peeled chilies
1 cup cooked tomatoes
2 T margarine
1 onion, finely chopped
  salt

Saute onion in margarine until golden brown. Add tomatoes and chilies. Simmer until thickened. Add yogurt, cheese, and salt; mix well. This sauce is good hot or cold on tortillas, pumpernickel or crisp wheat crackers.

## Bermuda Dressing

¼ cup finely chopped Bermuda onion
½ clove garlic, finely chopped
¼ cup finely chopped celery leaves
2 T finely chopped parsley
1 t salt
2 T tomato paste
1 cup yogurt

Combine all ingredients in a bowl and blend thoroughly. Makes about 1½ cups.

## Hollandaise Sauce

1 cup yogurt
4 egg yolks, beaten
1 T lemon juice
  dash hot pepper sauce
½ t salt

In top of small double boiler, mix all ingredients. Put over simmering water and cook, stirring vigorously, until smooth and thickened. Makes about 1½ cups. Delicious with broccoli, cauliflower or asparagus.

## Balkan Cooked Dressing

2 T honey
1 T flour
½ t salt
¼ t dry mustard
  dash cayenne
  pepper
2 eggs, beaten
½ cup yogurt
3 T vinegar

Mix honey, flour and seasonings in top part of small double boiler. Add remaining ingredients. Put over simmering water and cook, stirring, until thickened. Cool, then chill. Makes 1 cup of delicious dressing for cabbage or cooked vegetables.

## Simple Sauce

1 cup yogurt
  salt and pepper
2 t tomato sauce, for color

Mix well and serve on or separately with cooked vegetables.

## Lime Sauce

1 cup yogurt
1 clove garlic, minced
¼ t oregano
2 T olive oil
  salt
  pepper
  juice of 1 fresh lime

Blend together until smooth, yogurt, garlic, oregano, olive oil, seasonings, and lime juice. Serve with cold meats, fish, aspics or chilled vegetables. Lemon may be used in place of lime. Makes 1 cup.

## Tartar Sauce

½ cup yogurt
½ cup mayonnaise
2 T chopped pickle relish
2 T pimiento, finely chopped
2 T finely chopped parsley
1 T finely chopped green onion

Combine all ingredients and mix well. Serve hot or cold with fish fillets, cauliflower, broccoli or green beans. Makes 1½ cups.

## Cucumber Dressing

1½ cups yogurt
1 cucumber, finely chopped
1 clove garlic, minced
2 T finely chopped green onion

Blend all ingredients and refrigerate for several hours so the flavors will blend.

## Cottage Cheese Dressing

½ cup yogurt
½ cup cottage cheese
2 T vinegar or lemon juice
3 hard-cooked egg yolks
2 T finely chopped green pepper
1 T finely chopped chives
  salt

Mix all ingredients until well blended. Makes 1½ cups.

## Bleu Cheese Dressing

1 cup yogurt
1 cup bleu cheese
1 T chopped chives
1 T chopped parsley

Blend all ingredients. Use with green salads or as a spread for crackers. Makes 2 cups.

## Olive Dressing

½ cup finely chopped olives
1 t vinegar
  dash salt
1½ cups yogurt

Mix olives, vinegar and salt. Fold yogurt into mixture. Makes 1½ cups.

## French Cream Dressing

Stir 1/3 cup French dressing and ½ teaspoon salt into 2 cups yogurt. Ideal for vegetable salads. Makes 2 cups.

## Bombay Curry Sauce

1½ cup yogurt
2 T butter
1 t turmeric
1 t mustard seed
1 clove garlic, minced
2 t cumin seed
½ t cayenne
1/8 t cardamon
1 t salt
1 T minced green onion
1 T minced parsley

In a saucepan, melt butter and saute all ingredients except yogurt and salt. When mustard seeds have popped, remove pan from heat, and cool. Add yogurt and salt. Makes 1½ cups of sauce to be served with vegetables or meat.

## Bearnaise Sauce

4 egg yolks, beaten
1 cup yogurt
¼ cup white wine
¼ cup vinegar
1 T minced shallots
1 t dry tarragon
1 t chervil
2 T fresh minced tarragon or parsley

In a small saucepan, combine wine, vinegar, shallots, dry tarragon and chervil. Bring to boil and reduce liquid to practically a glaze. Place glaze and slightly beaten egg yolks in an enamel, glass or pottery container over hot water. Using a wisk, beat in yogurt a little at a time. Continue cooking and beating until sauce thickens (do not let water boil). Add fresh tarragon and serve immediately. Makes about 1 3/4 cups.

## Cooked Mint Sauce

2 cups yogurt
2 t cornstarch
½ t garlic powder
2 t dried mint

Mix cornstarch with enough water to make paste; add to yogurt and cook over low heat, stirring constantly. When boiling point is reached, add garlic powder and dried mint. This is an excellent sauce for squash. Makes 2 cups.

## Russian Caviar Dressing

½ cup yogurt
½ cup mayonnaise
3 T chili sauce
1 T finely chopped pimentos
1 t finely chopped chives
3 T caviar

Combine all the ingredients in a bowl and blend until smooth. Makes 1 2/3 cups.

## Oregano Dressing

1 cup yogurt
¼ cup honey
1 T lemon juice
2 T minced onion
1 T finely chopped parsley
1 t salt
½ t oregano

Mix all ingredients thoroughly and chill. Shake well before serving. Makes 1¾ cups.

# VEGETABLES

**Levant Eggplant**

*2 small eggplants,*
*   peeled and seeded*
*2 bell peppers,*
*   skinned and seeded*
*6 T olive oil*
*3 cups yogurt*
*1 clove garlic, pressed*
*   dash cayenne*
*   pinch powdered mint*
*1 t salt*
*¼ t pepper*

To peel pepper, cut in 2 inch lengthwise strips and put skin side up in a shallow baking pan. Place under hot broiler until pepper skin blisters, then peel. Mince peppers and finely chop eggplants. Saute together in oil until tender. Remove from heat and mash finely. Cool. In a bowl, mix all other ingredients and add the cooled eggplant mixture. Chill several hours or overnight. Serve very cold. May be used as a vegetable dish or a spread for crackers. Serves 6.

**Leeks with Cheese Sauce**

*1 lb. leeks*
*1½ cups yogurt*
*1 egg yolk*
*½ cup dry crumbs*
*1 T minced onion*
*½ cup butter*
*½ cup grated Monterey Jack cheese*
*1 T lemon juice*
*   cayenne and garlic salt*

Clean leeks and discard the outer leaves. Cut into 2 inch pieces and place in saucepan with small amount of water. Add salt and lemon juice; cook about 15 minutes. Remove from heat; drain. Melt butter in skillet; saute leeks for 2 minutes, adding onion the last minute. Arrange leeks in a shallow baking dish; sprinkle with garlic salt and cayenne. Beat yogurt and egg yolk; pour over leeks. Sprinkle with bread crumbs, then top with grated cheese. Cook under broiler until cheese is evenly browned. Serves 4.

## Avocado Stuffed Potatoes

*3 large baking potatoes*
*3 T butter*
*2/3 cup yogurt*
*½ cup finely chopped avocado*
  *salt and pepper*
*1 T finely chopped chives*
  *paprika*

Bake potatoes 450° for 45 minutes or until done. Slice in half lengthwise and scoop out pulp. Mash potato; add butter, chives, salt, pepper and yogurt. Mix well and fold in avocado. Pile mixture lightly in potato shells. Put in baking dish and sprinkle with paprika. Bake in oven for 10 minutes. Garnish with chopped chives. Serves 6.

## Serbian Peasant Green Beans

*2 lbs. fresh green beans*
*1 T finely chopped parsley*
*1 T finely chopped chives*
  *pinch dill weed*
*¼ t fennel*
*1 cup yogurt*
*2 T butter*
  *salt and pepper*
*4 slices bacon, cooked crisp*

Trim the beans, snap into halves and cook in small amount of water until just tender. Drain. Sprinkle the herbs over beans, add butter, salt and pepper; mix lightly. Pour yogurt over beans and mix well. Reheat and serve at once or chill and serve cold. Garnish with crumbled bacon. Serves 6.

## Eggplant Curry

*3 T oil*
*½ t cumin seed*
*1 t turmeric*
*½ t cayenne*
*1 eggplant, chopped with skin*
*1 onion, chopped*
*1 cup water*
*2 large tomatoes,*
  *peeled and chopped*
*1 cup yogurt*
*1 t salt*

Saute spices in hot oil; add chopped eggplant and onion. Stir until well coated, then add water and tomatoes. Cover and cook over low heat for 20 minutes. Stir in yogurt and salt. Reheat. Serves 6.

## Celery with Madeira

*2 cups celery, chopped*
*½ cup chicken stock*
*1 t honey*
*1 T flour*
*2 T butter*
*¼ cup Madeira*
*½ cup yogurt*
  *salt and pepper*

Put celery in a saucepan; add chicken stock, honey and seasonings. Cook for 5 minutes and set aside. In a small saucepan, heat butter and add flour. When well blended, pour in Madeira and mix until smooth. Add wine mixture to celery and bring to a boil, stirring constantly. Remove from heat and stir in yogurt. Reheat and serve with your favorite chicken recipe. Serves 4.

## Green Beans Byzantine

1 cup mushrooms
2 T butter
2 cups green beans, cooked
1/3 cup yogurt
¼ t salt
2 t chopped parsley or basil

Saute mushrooms in butter. Add beans, yogurt and salt. Heat and serve garnished with parsley or basil. Serves 4.

## Mrs. Feeney's Turnips

2 lbs. turnips
2 T butter
½ cup yogurt
2 T rum or sherry
  salt

Peel and wash turnips. Chop, then cook in small amount of water over low heat until tender. Mash fine and add salt, butter, yogurt and spirits. Reheat and serve at once. Serves 4.

## Ginger Cauliflower

1 cauliflower
1 cup yogurt
1 t honey
1 t finely grated ginger root
2 T butter
  dash garlic salt
  salt

Wash cauliflower; remove the core and separate into tiny flowerlets. Mix yogurt, honey, garlic salt, ginger root and salt in a deep bowl. Add cauliflower and let stand for 2 or 3 hours. Heat butter in a large frying pan; add cauliflower mixture and simmer slowly until tender. Serves 4.

## Baghdad Bell Peppers

3 large bell peppers
1 cup yogurt
2 T olive oil
½ t salt

Cut stems from peppers and then halve them. Remove seeds and place under hot broiler until skins blister; let cool and peel off the skins. Heat the olive oil and lightly saute pieces of pepper. Put in a bowl; add yogurt, salt and remaining oil from the pan. Mix well and serve hot or chilled. Makes 4 servings.

## Brussels Sprouts Monterey

1 lb. Brussels sprouts
¾ cup yogurt
2 T butter
¼ t paprika
  dash garlic salt
  pepper

Cook sprouts in small amount of water until tender. Drain and add remaining ingredients. Place over low heat and stir gently until reheated. Makes 4 servings.

## Brussels Sprouts Casserole

1½ lbs. Brussels sprouts, steamed
1 cup stewed tomatoes
½ cup grated cheddar cheese
1 cup yogurt
2 t flour
¼ cup chopped almonds

Arrange Brussels sprouts in oiled casserole and cover with tomatoes. Mix yogurt, flour and grated cheese together; spoon over sprouts. Cover and bake at 350º for 15 minutes. Garnish with chopped almonds. Serves 4 to 6.

## Curried Carrots

*2 cups thinly sliced carrots*
*1 t salt*
*¼ cup water*
*3 T butter*
*¼ t cardamon*
*1 t turmeric*
*¼ t ground fenugreek*
*1 t mustard seed*
*1 t cumin seed*
*1 clove garlic, chopped*
*¼ t cayenne*
*1 cup yogurt*
*1 T flour*

Cook carrots in salted water. Set aside. In a saucepan, heat butter and add spices. Stir until well blended. Pour spices into carrots. Mix flour and yogurt until smooth; add to carrot mixture. Let simmer over low heat 10 minutes. Serves 4.

## Savory Spinach

*1 lb. fresh spinach*
*1 onion, finely chopped*
*4 T margarine*
*1 cup yogurt*
  *salt and pepper*

Put washed and chopped spinach in a large saucepan; using only the water that clings to the leaves to cook the spinach. Cover and cook over medium heat until spinach has wilted. Remove from heat and set aside. In a small pan, saute onion in margarine until tender. Drain water from spinach and add the spinach to onion. Saute for a few minutes, remove from heat and cool. Add salt and pepper to yogurt and pour over cooled spinach. Mix well and chill. Also good served hot. Serves 4.

## Romanian Baked Mushrooms

*1 lb. large mushrooms,*
  *thinly sliced*
*3 T olive oil*
*1 large onion, finely minced*
*2 t flour*
*½ cup milk*
*1 cup yogurt*
*1 T minced parsley*
  *pinch nutmeg*
*½ cup grated cheese, sharp cheddar*
  *butter*
  *salt and pepper*

Heat oil and lightly saute onions until soft. Add mushrooms and continue cooking slowly, stirring frequently. When most of the moisture has disappeared, sprinkle in flour and continue stirring until remaining liquid thickens. In a mixing bowl, blend milk and yogurt; add salt, pepper, parsley and nutmeg. Add the mixture to mushrooms and pour into an attractive shallow baking dish. Top with grated cheese and dot with butter. Place the dish in a baking tin with about ½ inch of hot water at the bottom. Bake at 350° until the top has browned. Serves 4 to 6.

## Parsleyed Parsnips

*2 lbs. parsnips*
*1 cup yogurt*
*3 T butter*
*3 T minced parsley*
  *salt and pepper*

Clean and scrape parsnips. Cut in half lengthwise and remove core if tough. Cook in salted water 10 minutes. Remove from heat and drain. Saute parsnips in butter for 6 to 8 minutes. Arrange parsnips in a hot serving dish; pour over beaten yogurt and garnish with parsley. Serve immediately. Serves 6.

## Unbeatable Beets

¼ cup boiling water
3 cups grated raw beets
  beet tops, shredded
1/8 t basil
1 bay leaf
  salt
2 t honey
2/3 cup yogurt

To boiling water, add basil, bay leaf, beets and beet tops. Cover and simmer 5 minutes. Remove bay leaf and add salt to taste. Cool, then add yogurt and honey. Chill before serving or reheat and serve hot. Makes 4 to 6 servings.

## Beets with Horseradish

3 cups cooked, sliced beets
½ cup yogurt
2 t flour
1 T prepared horseradish
1 T chopped chives
1 t grated onion
  salt

Whip together yogurt and flour. In double boiler, mix all other ingredients and heat. Add yogurt mixture and reheat.

## Golden Cabbage

6 cups finely chopped cabbage
3 T margarine
2 t cumin seed
1 t turmeric
½ cup yogurt
1 t salt

Heat margarine and seasonings; add cabbage and stir until all is well coated. Cook gently for about 5 minutes. Add yogurt, stirring until reheated. Serves 6.

## Country Fried Tomatoes

6 large beefsteak tomatoes, half ripe
  salt and pepper
  garlic salt
  fine, dry crumbs
¼ cup butter
1 T flour
½ t basil
½ t paprika
1½ cups yogurt
2 green onions, finely chopped

Cut tomatoes in ¾ inch slices. Season with salt, pepper and garlic salt and then coat with crumbs. Melt 2 tablespoons butter in large skillet. Saute tomatoes quickly on both sides, turning carefully. Add more butter as needed. Remove tomatoes to a hot platter. In same skillet, add 1 teaspoon salt, flour, basil and paprika. Stir well and add yogurt slowly. Over low heat, cook until thickens. Pour over tomatoes and garnish with green onions. Serves 6.

## Tomatoes Italiano

6 medium tomatoes
½ cup bread crumbs
  garlic dressing
¾ cup yogurt, drained
¼ cup grated cheese
  salt and pepper

Slice off tops of tomatoes and scoop out pulp. Moisten bread crumbs with garlic dressing. Combine tomato pulp, bread crumbs, yogurt, grated cheese, salt and pepper. Mix well. Fill tomato shells with mixture and place in oiled baking dish. Top with grated cheese. Bake in 375º oven for 15 to 20 minutes. Serves 6.

## Cabin Style Lima Beans

*2 cups dried baby lima beans, cooked*
*¼ cup molasses*
*1 cup yogurt*
*1 T minced onion*
*½ t dry mustard*
*1/8 t pepper*
*1 t salt*
*1 t Worcestershire sauce*
*3 slices bacon*

Drain beans, saving ½ cup liquid. Combine all ingredients except bacon. Place bean mixture in casserole dish and arrange bacon slices on top. Bake in 325º oven 1 hour. Serves 8.

## Baked Summer Squash

*2 lbs. summer squash*
*½ cup grated cheddar cheese*
*¾ cup yogurt*
  *garlic salt*
*3 T melted butter*

Slice summer squash in half and place in large shallow baking dish. Brush with melted butter and sprinkle with garlic salt. Spoon yogurt over squash and cover with grated cheese. Bake in 400º oven until cheese is melted and lightly browned. Do not over cook; squash should be crunchy. Serves 4 to 6.

## Vegetable Mosaic

*1 cup cooked green beans, chopped*
*1 cup cooked diced carrots*
*1 cup cooked peas*
*1 cup cooked diced potatoes*
*¾ cup chopped celery*
*1/3 cup chopped parsley*
*2 T minced onion*
*½ cup yogurt*
*1/3 cup mayonnaise*
*1 T vinegar*
*1 t salt*
  *pepper*

In a large bowl, lightly combine vegetables. Blend together yogurt, mayonnaise, vinegar, salt and pepper. Add to vegetables and toss. Chill thoroughly. Makes 8 servings.

## Broiled Tomatoes

*4 tomatoes*
  *salt*
  *pepper*
*1/3 cup yogurt*
*1/3 cup mayonnaise*
*1/8 t curry powder*
*¼ cup bread crumbs*
  *butter*

Wash tomatoes and cut in half cross-wise. Sprinkle with salt and pepper. Blend together yogurt, mayonnaise and curry powder; spread on cut side of tomatoes. Sprinkle with bread crumbs and dot with butter. Broil until mixture is bubbly, about 5 to 10 minutes. Serves 8.

## Zucchini Supreme

3 medium zucchini, chopped
1/3 cup yogurt
2 T butter
1 T grated Parmesan cheese
½ t salt
1/8 t paprika
1 egg yolk
1 T chopped chives
  bread crumbs

Simmer zucchini in small amount of water for about 6 to 8 minutes. Shake the pan to prevent sticking. Drain zucchini well and set aside. In a saucepan combine yogurt, butter, grated cheese, salt and paprika. Stir mixture over low heat until hot. Remove from heat and stir in egg yolk and chives. Add zucchini. Place mixture in a baking dish, cover top with bread crumbs, dot with butter and sprinkle with more cheese. Brown under broiler. Serves 4.

## Zucchini Zoltan

1½ lbs. zucchini, thinly sliced
¼ cup white wine
½ cup stock
2 cups yogurt
1 egg yolk
¼ cup fresh dill, minced

Simmer zucchini in wine and stock for 5 minutes. Cool. Blend together yogurt, egg yolk and dill. Drain zucchini and add yogurt mixture. When well mixed, chill. Serves 6.

## Roasted Eggplant

2 small eggplants
1 clove garlic, minced
1 cup yogurt
  salt and pepper

Place eggplants on charcoal grill, turning frequently until tender, about 10 minutes, (outsides will be charred). Cool briefly and then peel off skins with fingers. Place peeled eggplants on hot platter and chop into small pieces. Add remaining ingredients; mix thoroughly. Serve as a side dish with kebabs. Serves 4 to 6.

## Onions ala Baba

6 onions, chopped
3 T butter
1 cup yogurt
½ cup milk
3 egg yolks
½ cup grated cheese
¼ cup bread crumbs

Simmer onions in milk and butter for 20 minutes over low heat. Drain and place in oiled baking dish. In a bowl, mix egg yolks, yogurt, cheese and seasonings. Pour mixture over onions; top with bread crumbs and bake at 350º for 20 minutes. Serves 6.

# FISH, MEAT & GAME

## Broiled Butter Fish

6 butter fish
2½ T oil
1 t mustard seed
1 t minced onion
1 cup yogurt
½ t salt
1 large red onion, quartered and sliced
2 T vinegar
 dash pepper
 pinch dry mustard
 pimiento strips

Clean fish and dry with paper towels. Heat 1½ tablespoons oil in a heavy skillet, add mustard seed. When seeds pop, add minced onion and saute until tender. Cool. Combine mixture with yogurt and salt; spread over fish, cover and marinate one hour. In a shallow bowl, combine vinegar, 1 tablespoon oil, dry mustard, salt and pepper. Mix in red onion slices and allow to marinate one hour. Grill fish over hot coals about 5 minutes on each side. Drain onions; garnish fish with onions and pimiento. Arrange fish on a platter with parsley and lime slices. Serves 6.

## Gourmet Sea Scallops

1½ lbs. scallops
1½ cups dry white wine
 salt and pepper
2 T oil
1 T butter
1 T flour
1 cup yogurt
½ cup milk
½ cup chopped mushrooms
2 T grated Swiss cheese
2 T bread crumbs

Combine scallops, wine, salt and pepper in large heavy saucepan. Cover. Bring to a boil over low heat and simmer gently for 5 minutes. Drain and set aside liquid. Remove and chop scallops. In same saucepan, heat oil and add flour, stirring in cooking liquid and milk, a little at a time. Mix thoroughly, then add yogurt, scallops and mushrooms. Cook for 5 minutes, stirring occasionally. Remove from heat; add Swiss cheese. Fill buttered casserole with scallop mixture. Sprinkle with bread crumbs, dot with butter and place under broiler to brown. Serves 4 to 6.

## Yogurt Baked Fish Cake

*3½ cups hot mashed potatoes*
*1 egg, beaten*
*2 cups cooked fish*
*1 green pepper, minced*
*1 onion, minced*
*2 T butter*
*1 T minced parsley*
*1½ cups yogurt*
  *chopped chives*

In a saucepan, saute onion and pepper in butter 2 minutes; remove from heat and add fish, parsley and yogurt. Mix egg with mashed potatoes and pour half of potato mixture into baking dish. Spread all of fish mixture over potatoes. Top with remaining potatoes and garnish with chopped chives. Bake 15 to 20 minutes in 350⁰ oven. Serves 6.

## Cod Fish with Mushrooms

*2 lbs. cod fish, fillets or steaks*
*6 T oil*
*¼ lb. mushroom caps, thinly sliced*
*¼ cup butter*
*1 cup yogurt*
*1 T flour*
  *salt*

Sprinkle fish with salt. Put oil in baking dish, add the pieces of fish, turn over to coat with oil. Bake in 400⁰ oven until tender. Heat butter; add mushroom slices and saute until tender. When fish is done, cover with mushrooms. Blend flour with yogurt until smooth and pour over the top of fish and mushrooms. Return to oven and continue cooking for about 15 minutes. Serves 6.

## Stuffed Fillet of Sole

*1½ lbs. fillet of sole*
*2 T finely chopped onion*
*2 T butter*
*1½ cups soft bread crumbs*
*1 T chopped parsley*
*¼ t marjoram*
*¼ t salt*
*2 T flour*
*1 cup yogurt*
*1½ cups milk*
  *pepper*

*For Sauce:*
*2 T butter*
*2 T flour*
*1 T finely chopped pimiento*
*1/8 t ground marjoram*
*¾ cup yogurt*
*½ t salt*
*1 t parsley*

Saute onions in butter until lightly browned. Remove from heat; add bread crumbs, parsley, yogurt, marjoram and salt. Mix well and spread over fillets. Roll up and fasten with tooth picks. Place in shallow baking pan, add milk and sprinkle with pepper and salt. Bake 30 minutes in 350⁰ oven. Drain milk from fish, then return sole to oven to keep warm.

For sauce, mix butter and flour in saucepan. Heat and gradually add milk drained from fillets. Stir vigorously over medium heat until sauce thickens. Remove from heat and add yogurt, salt, parsley, marjoram and pimiento. Serve over fish. Serves 6.

## Sherry Creamed Chicken

½ cup butter
1½ cups chicken stock
1 cup yogurt
¼ cup sherry
1 cup green peas, cooked
2 T chopped green pepper or
  red sweet pepper
4 T flour
1 cup cooked, chopped chicken
1 cup sliced mushrooms
  dash cayenne
  salt

Saute mushrooms and peppers in 4 tablespoons butter until lightly browned. Set aside. In another pan, blend flour and 4 tablespoons butter. Add seasonings and cook over low heat until bubbling. Remove from heat, add stock. Stir well. Beat yogurt and blend in gradually. Bring to boiling point, stirring constantly, about 1 minute. Add chicken, peas, mushrooms and peppers. Reheat, then add sherry just before serving. Spoon over toast or rice. Serves 4.

## Ginger Lime Chicken

1 frying chicken, cut up
1 cup yogurt
1 clove garlic, minced
1½ t freshly grated ginger
¼ cup lime juice
1 t ground coriander
1 t cumin
¼ t cayenne
¼ t powdered aniseed
¼ cup oil

Mix all ingredients except oil. Marinate chicken in this sauce for 24 hours or longer. Keep refrigerated. Put chicken on greased rack in a baking pan and roast at 375º, basting occasionally with oil until tender. Serve with wedges of lime. Makes 4 servings.

72

## Chicken Paprika

2 frying chickens, cut up
  salt and pepper
4 onions, sliced thin
3 T butter
2 T paprika
1 cup chicken stock
2 cups yogurt
2 T flour
  cooked noodles

Rub chicken with salt and pepper. In Dutch oven, saute onions in butter until limp. Stir in paprika; add chicken and brown quickly over medium heat. Add stock; cover and bake in 350º over for 1 hour. Remove chicken from Dutch oven and stir yogurt and flour into sauce. Return chicken, cover and bake 20 minutes longer. Serve with hot noodles. Serves 6 to 8.

## Old Country Chicken

1 large chicken
  juice 1 lemon
¼ t cloves
½ t cinnamon
6 T olive oil
6 tomatoes, peeled and chopped
¼ cup tomato sauce
1½ cups hot water
  salt and pepper

Clean and cut chicken into serving pieces. Stir lemon juice, cloves, cinnamon, salt and pepper together and rub each piece of chicken with mixture. Heat oil in large frying pan and brown the chicken pieces. Remove chicken from frying pan, but keep hot. Add tomatoes and tomato sauce to the pan, stir well, gradually adding hot water. Cook over a gentle heat until tomatoes are soft and the sauce is thick. Return the chicken pieces to the pan. Turn each piece over and over until coated with sauce. Cover pan and cook over medium heat until chicken is very tender. Serves 4.

## Caravan Chicken

2 fryers, disjointed
2 cups yogurt
3 t salt
2 T butter
2 cloves garlic, minced
1 t grated ginger
1 bell pepper, thinly sliced
1 onion, halved and thinly sliced
2 t turmeric
4 t coriander
¼ t cloves
¼ t cinnamon
¼ t pepper
1/8 t cardamon
1 T grated coconut
2 tomatoes, halved and sliced

Marinate chicken in yogurt overnight. Add 2 teaspoons salt and put in a Dutch oven. Cook covered, over low heat for 50 minutes or until tender. Turn heat to high; uncover and cook until marinade thickens. In a skillet, melt butter and saute garlic, ginger, green pepper and onion 3 minutes, stirring constantly. Add turmeric, coriander, remaining teaspoon salt, cloves, cinnamon, pepper, cardamon and coconut. Cook over low heat 10 minutes. Stir frequently. Add tomatoes, cook 3 minutes. Stir mixture into the chicken and cook 10 minutes, uncovered. Garnish with additional coconut. Serves 6 to 8.

## Chicken Bulgarian

1 fryer chicken
1 cup yogurt
1½ t salt
1 clove garlic, minced
½ t ground cardamon
1 t chili powder
¼ t cinnamon
2 T flour

Combine yogurt, salt, garlic, cardamon, chili powder and cinnamon. Marinate chicken in yogurt mixture for at least 4 hours ( overnight is best). Place chicken in baking pan, skin side up. Combine flour with marinade and spoon over chicken. Bake about 1½ hours or until tender in 350º oven. Baste occasionally with marinade. Serves 4.

## Iranian Kebabs

2 lbs. lean lamb,
  cut in 1 inch cubes
1 cup yogurt
1 t salt
1 cup chopped onion

Mix yogurt, onion and salt. Put meat into this marinade and refrigerate for 2 days, turning occasionally. Thread meat on skewers and broil, preferably over charcoal, until brown on the outside, but juicy within. Serves 6 with rice.

## Lamb Shanks with Pearl Onions

*4 lamb shanks, cut in thirds*
*¼ t garlic salt*
*1 t salt*
  *pepper*
*¼ cup oil*
*1½ cups beef stock*
*1 cup yogurt*
*8 small carrots, whole*
*1 can pearl onions, drained*

Combine flour, salt, pepper and garlic salt in a bowl. Coat lamb shanks with flour mixture. Heat oil in large heavy skillet; add meat and brown slowly, turning frequently. Remove meat. Sprinkle 1 tablespoon of the seasoned flour in skillet and mix until smooth. Gradually add 1 cup of stock, stirring vigorously over moderate heat until sauce thickens. Add browned meat and cover. Simmer over low heat until meat is tender, about 1½ hours. During the last 20 mintues, add carrots. If sauce becomes too thick during cooking, add remaining stock. Remove meat and carrots from skillet and skim off all fat from sauce. Blend together yogurt and 1 tablespoon flour. Gradually pour yogurt into meat sauce, mixing thoroughly and cook over low heat until thickened. Add meat, onions and carrots. Reheat. Serves 4.

## Roast Lamb with Macedonia Sauce

*½ leg lamb, about 4 lbs.*
*1 clove garlic*
  *flour*
*1 t honey*
*2 T margarine, melted*
*3 bay leaves*
*1 onion, finely chopped*
*½ cup wine vinegar*
*1½ cups yogurt*
  *dill weed*
  *pepper*
  *salt*

For basting sauce, combine ¼ t salt, margarine, bay leaves, onion, vinegar and honey. Wipe lamb with a damp cloth. Rub on all sides with garlic. Put a thin coat of flour on lamb and place meat on a rack in 450º oven for 30 minutes, basting from time to time. Reduce heat to 350º and roast about 2 hours longer, (or until meat thermometer registers 185º). Remove roast to hot platter. Rinse pan thoroughly with ½ cup water and strain drippings into a saucepan. Add yogurt and heat gently. Season with salt, pepper and dill. Serve with lamb. Serves 6.

## Oasis Lamb

1½ cups yogurt
2 lbs. lamb, cubed
3 onions, chopped
¼ lb. dried prunes
3 T butter
1½ T flour
¼ cup plum wine
¼ t paprika
 salt
1 cup water

Saute onions in butter until transparent; add salt, paprika and lamb. When lamb is lightly browned, add water and prunes. Cover and simmer over low heat until meat is tender. Add more water if necessary. Mix flour, wine and a little water until smooth. Pour into meat mixture, stirring until sauce thickens. Remove from heat and add yogurt. Reheat and serve with rice. Makes 6 servings.

## Turk Kebabs

1½ lbs. lamb
1 onion, chopped
 salt and pepper
6 slices wheat bread
2 cups meat stock or broth
2 cups yogurt
½ t paprika
2 T melted butter

Rub meat well with onion, salt and pepper. Cut into chunks about 1 inch square. Toast bread until crisp and brown. Place toast on a large serving platter; add meat stock and put into a warm oven. The bread will absorb all the broth; if any remains, pour it off. Thread meat on oiled skewers and grill over hot charcoal. When meat is ready, divide it equally on top of each slice of toast and return to oven. Put yogurt in a saucepan and stir until warm. Add a little salt and pour over meat. Stir paprika into butter and pour hot over the yogurt as a garnish. Serves 6.

## East Indian Lamb Curry

2 lbs. lamb
2 t salt
½ cup margarine
1 large onion, chopped
¼ t chili powder
1 t ground coriander
1 t ground ginger
4 whole cardamons
4 cloves
2 sticks cinnamon
½ t peppercorns
1 clove garlic, finely chopped
1 cup yogurt

Sprinkle lamb with salt. In large skillet, saute lamb and onions until lightly browned. Remove and reserve. In same pan add chili powder, coriander and ginger. Cook for a minute or two; add lamb, onions, whole spices, yogurt and garlic. Cover and simmer for 2 hours or until meat is tender. If sauce becomes dry, add a little water. Serves 6.

## Curried Lamb Chops

6 lamb loin chops, 1 inch thick
2 cups yogurt
½ t coriander
2 T poppy seeds, crushed
¼ t ground allspice
1 small clove garlic, crushed
1 t salt
1 T grated fresh ginger
½ cup butter

Combine yogurt with coriander, poppy seeds, allspice, garlic, salt and ginger. Spread on both sides of chops and let stand for several hours. Remove from marinade and saute in butter until brown on both sides. Pour marinade into pan and simmer until meat is tender. Serves 6.

## Lamb Shanks with Capers

6 lamb shanks
2 T melted butter
2 T flour
½ t salt
½ t paprika
  freshly ground pepper
1 cup lamb stock
½ cup yogurt
1 small bottle capers, drained

Simmer lamb shanks in salted water until tender, 2 to 2½ hours. Reserve stock. Blend together butter, flour, salt paprika and pepper. Slowly add lamb stock. Bring to boil stirring constantly. Cook until smooth; add yogurt and capers. Spoon over well-drained lamb shanks and serve at once. Serves 6.

## Gourmet Cutlets

1 lb. veal cutlets
¼ cup butter
1 onion, finely chopped
1 T poppy seed
¼ cup dry white wine
2 cups yogurt
3 slices lemon
  garlic salt
  pepper

Cut meat into 1 inch cubes; season with salt and pepper and marinate in wine 4 hours. Remove and wipe carefully. In a skillet, saute veal in butter for 5 minutes. Add onion, lemon slices and poppy seed; saute another 5 minutes, stirring continuously. Remove the veal and keep hot. Add the wine marinade, bring to boil and reduce amount by 1/4. Strain sauce; add to beaten yogurt. Pour into baking dish; add veal, cover and bake in 350º oven 45 minutes. Serves 4.

## Savory Veal

2 lbs. cubed lean veal shoulder
  salt
  pepper
  flour
3 T oil
½ cup hot water
1 onion, sliced
½ cup mushrooms, sliced
1 cup buttermilk
1 cup yogurt

Sprinkle veal with salt and pepper. Roll in flour. Saute in oil until brown on both sides. Add water, onion and mushrooms; cover and cook over low heat until tender, adding more water if needed. Blend together buttermilk and yogurt until smooth. Add 3 tablespoons flour to small amount of yogurt mixture, stirring to a smooth paste. Add remaining yogurt mixture to paste; stir well and pour over veal. Cook over low heat, stirring constantly until thickened. Serve with rice. Yields 6 portions.

## Veal Loaf

1½ lbs. ground veal
2 cups grated raw carrots
1 onion, finely chopped
1 3 oz. can chopped mushrooms, drained
½ cup dry bread crumbs
1 t salt
¼ t pepper
1 cup yogurt

Mix all ingredients in a bowl. When thoroughly mixed, press into a greased loaf pan. Bake in 375º oven about 1½ hours. Remove from oven and let stand 10 minutes. Pour off any liquid and turn loaf out on hot platter. Serves 6 to 8.

## Nomad Kebab

2 lbs. top sirloin or leg of lamb,
  cut in 1 inch cubes
1 cup yogurt
2 t coriander
1 T poppy seed
1 t ginger
1 t turmeric
¼ t cumin seed
¼ t cardamon
1 clove garlic
2 t salt
¼ t pepper
1 onion, chopped
½ lb. fresh mushrooms
1 qt. cherry tomatoes
2 bell peppers, cut in chunks
¼ cup oil

Cover meat with boiling water and let soak 5 to 10 minutes; drain well. Combine all ingredients except fresh vegetables and oil. Spread mixture over meat cubes and let marinate 1 hour or more. Put meat on skewers alternating with mushrooms, tomatoes and bell pepper chunks. Cook over hot coals 10 to 12 minutes, brushing with oil and turning occasionally. Serves 6 to 8.

## Yogurt Burgers

1 lb. ground beef
1 t salt
  pepper
1 onion, finely chopped
½ cup wheat germ
1 cup yogurt
¾ cup fine dry bread crumbs

Mix beef, salt, pepper, onion and wheat germ together in large bowl. Add yogurt gradually, beating constantly. Add bread crumbs and mix thoroughly. Shape into patties and place in shallow baking pan. Bake in 375º oven until done. Makes 6 patties.

## Tangy Braised Beef Cubes

1½ lbs. round steak, cubed
1 t salt
  pepper
1 t garlic salt
  flour
1 can tomatoes
1 cup yogurt

Combine salt, pepper, garlic salt and ¼ cup flour in in a clean paper bag. Add meat and shake until well coated. Using heavy skillet, brown meat slowly in oil turning to brown on all sides. Add tomatoes; stir well and cover. Simmer 2 hours or until meat is tender. Stir often during cooking. Add water if mixture becomes too dry. Mix 2 tablespoons flour with yogurt and stir until smooth. Add to meat a few mintues before serving and cook stirring constantly until sauce thickens. Serves 6.

## Almond Meat Balls

1 lb. ground beef
2 T finely chopped parsley
1 t salt
1 small onion, finely chopped
2 eggs, beaten
½ cup yogurt
  margarine
4 oz. almonds, ground
1 t turmeric
2 t lime juice
½ cup dry bread crumbs

Mix ground beef with parsley, onion, salt, eggs and yogurt. Form into small meat balls and roll in bread crumbs. Saute in margarine until well browned. Cover and continue cooking over low heat until done. Make a paste of almonds, turmeric and a little water. Add paste to meat balls; cover and shake a few times. Serve with lime juice sprinkled over the meat balls. Serves 4.

## Stuffed Grape Leaves

¾ lb. minced lamb or beef
1 onion, finely chopped
3 T olive oil
6 T rice, uncooked
¼ cup pine nuts
2 T chopped dill
  pinch mint
  dash cinnamon
1 lb. grape leaves
½ cup white wine
1½ cups meat stock
1 cup yogurt
1 clove garlic, minced

Clean and wash grape leaves; drop into boiling salted water and cook 3 minutes; drain well pressing out all water. Cut large leaves in half down the center vein. Saute onions in oil until limp; add rice and cook until golden. Add pine nuts and toast for 1 minute; remove from heat and add meat, mint, dill, cinnamon, salt and pepper. Put 1 tablespoon of mixture on each leaf half and roll into finger shape, tucking in the edges. Put the rolls in a casserole, cover with meat stock and wine. Cook for 45 minutes over medium heat. Add more stock if needed. Serve on hot platter, topped with blend of yogurt, mint and minced garlic. Serves 4.

## Egyptian Cabbage Rolls

1 small head cabbage
½ lb. ground beef
½ lb. ground pork
1 T finely minced onion
1 cup cooked rice
  pinch nutmeg
1 t salt
  dash garlic salt
¼ t dry mustard
1 8 oz. can tomato sauce
1½ cups yogurt
1½ T flour
  chopped chives or dill
  cooked noodles with butter
  and dill seed

Blanch cabbage in boiling water 5 minutes. Cool slightly; remove leaves carefully and cut out coarse veins. Mix onion, meat, rice, nutmeg, pepper, salt, garlic salt, dry mustard and just enough tomato sauce to moisten. Place heaping tablespoon of filling in center of each leaf; tuck ends over filling and roll. Place rolls in large shallow baking dish. Mix flour with yogurt and pour over rolls. Cover dish with foil; bake in 375º oven for 1½ hours. Remove foil after 1 hour. Garnish with chives and serve with noodles. Serves 4.

## Hearty Western Meat Balls

1 lb. ground beef
1 cup soft bread crumbs
1 egg
¼ cup milk
1 T minced onion
1 t grated lemon rind
½ t pepper
3 T butter
½ green pepper chopped
3 T flour
1 1 lb. can tomatoes
1 cup yogurt
¼ t seasoned salt

Mix ground beef with bread crumbs, egg, milk, onion, lemon rind, garlic, salt and pepper. Shape into walnut sized balls and brown on all sides in 2 tablespoons butter. Remove meat balls. Add remaining 1 tablespoon butter to drippings in same skillet. Add green pepper and cook 2 or 3 minutes. Blend in flour and stir in tomatoes and seasoned salt. Put meat balls back in skillet. Bring to a boil; cover and simmer over low heat for 25 minutes, stirring occasionally. Add yogurt; reheat. Serves 4.

## Armenian Hash

1 lb. ground meat
3 medium potatoes,
  boiled in jackets
1 onion, finely chopped
1 egg, beaten
1 t cumin
½ cup yogurt
  oil

Peel boiled potatoes and chop in small cubes. Mix meat, potatoes, onion and cumin. Blend together yogurt and egg; add to meat mixture. Toss lightly until well mixed. Shape into patties and saute in oil until done. Serves 4.

## Dried Beef in Cheese Sauce

¼ lb. dried beef
¼ cup margarine
2 T minced onion
3 T flour
1 cup milk
1 cup yogurt
1 3 oz. can mushrooms, drained
1 cup shredded cheddar cheese
2 T chopped parsley
  salt and pepper

Cut beef in julienne strips. Add beef and onions to margarine in saucepan. Saute 2 or 3 minutes. Blend in flour. Gradually add milk. Cook until thickened, stirring constantly. Add yogurt, mushrooms, cheddar cheese, parsley, salt and pepper. Heat and serve over English muffins, rice, toast or in pop-overs. Serves 4.

## Avocado Beef Dinner

1½ lbs. ground beef
1 onion, chopped
½ t salt
½ t garlic salt
1 t pepper
1 10½ oz. can cream
  of mushroom soup
1 cup yogurt
1 avocado, cubed
½ avocado, sliced
3 cups hot steamed rice

In a large skillet, lightly brown beef. Add onion, salt, garlic salt and pepper. Cover and cook over low heat about 30 minutes. Blend in soup and cook another 5 minutes. Fold in yogurt and cubed avocado. Reheat. Garnish with avocado slices dipped in lemon juice and serve with hot rice. Serves 4 to 6.

## Swedish Meat Balls

1 lb. ground beef
1 lb. ground veal
½ cup soaked whole barley or rye
1 cup yogurt
1 egg, slightly beaten
3 T grated onion
¼ t allspice
½ t pepper
1 t salt
3 T oil
2 cups beef stock
2 T flour
¼ onion salt

Combine beef, veal, barley or rye, ½ cup yogurt, egg, onion, 1/8 teaspoon allspice, pepper and salt. Shape into balls and brown well in oil. Pour stock over meat balls. Cover and simmer over low heat ½ hour. Remove meat balls from skillet. In a bowl, mix remaining ½ cup yogurt, flour, 1/8 teaspoon allspice and onion salt. Add yogurt mixture to stock in skillet, stirring vigorously. Cook over low heat, stirring until thickened. Add meat balls and reheat. Serves 6.

## Rabbit Stew

2 lb. jointed rabbit
2 T olive oil
1 large onion, chopped
1½ T flour
1½ cups yogurt
1½ cups meat stock
  salt and pepper

Season rabbit; put in a large skillet with olive oil and onion. Brown lightly and place in a casserole dish. Pour over stock. Cover and cook slowly for 1½ hours or until tender. Thicken gravy with flour and add yogurt. Cook over very low heat 5 minutes and serve. Serves 4.

## Tongue Mousse

1 T unflavored gelatin
¼ cup water
1 12 oz. can vichyssoise
1 T horseradish
¼ cup yogurt
1 12 oz. can tongue, diced
1 pimiento, chopped
3 T chopped parsley
  watercress

Sprinkle gelatin on ¼ cup cold water. Dissolve gelatin over hot water. Add remaining ingredients except watercress and turn into a 1 quart mold. Chill until set. Unmold on a bed of watercress. Serves 4.

## Beef Stroganoff

2 lbs. lean sirloin steak
3 T butter
2 onions, sliced thin
1 lb. mushrooms, sliced
1 T flour
¼ t pepper
½ t paprika
  dash cayenne
1 cup yogurt

Cut beef across grain into narrow strips. Heat 2 tablespoons butter in heavy skillet and add meat and onions. Cook over high heat a few minutes, turning meat to brown on all sides. Lower heat; add mushrooms and more butter if needed and cook covered for 10 minutes. Remove mixture to top of double boiler and place over boiling water to keep hot. To skillet juices, add remaining tablespoon butter and stir in flour and seasonings. Pour in yogurt slowly, blending to keep smooth. Add meat mixture and heat only until mixture is again hot. Serve with noodles or rice and garnish with chives or dill. Serves 6.

## Pork and Cabbage Dinner

2 lbs. pork shoulder
1 head cabbage, shredded
¼ cup oil
2 chopped onions
  salt and pepper
1 T paprika
1 cup yogurt

Cut meat in stew-size cubes. Heat half the oil, saute half the onions until golden brown; add the cabbage and cook until tender. In another pan heat remaining oil; saute the rest of the onions; add meat and continue cooking until brown. Cover and simmer over low heat about 10 minutes. Add cooked cabbage; stir well and add salt and pepper. Cook together for another 20 minutes. Remove from heat and add yogurt.

## Beer Stew

3 lbs. boneless pot roast,
  cut in 1½ inch cubes
2 T oil
4 onions, chopped
1 t flour
1 t honey
1 cup beer
¼ cup consomme
1 cup yogurt
1 bay leaf
½ t pepper
  salt

Heat oil in large, heavy pan. Add meat and brown well on all sides. Remove and reserve. Add onions to pan and saute lightly. Stir in flour and honey, mix well and cook until browned. Blend together consomme, beer and yogurt and stir into onion mixture. Continue to stir until boiling. Add meat, salt, pepper and bay leaf. Cover tightly and simmer 2½ to 3 hours or until meat is tender. Serves 6.

## Salmi of Wild Duck

1 duck
½ cup port
½ cup stock
2 T butter
2 T flour
½ cup cognac
½ cup yogurt
1 t lemon juice
  salt
  pepper
½ cup skinned chestnuts

Roast duck in 450° oven 30 minutes, basting every 5 minutes with juice from pan. Remove duck and keep warm. Add stock to drippings and strain. In a saucepan, heat butter and flour; add port, salt, pepper and strained juices. Cook until reduced by one-half. Remove from heat and add beaten yogurt and lemon juice; reheat. Fillet the duck; pour cognac over and ignite. Arrange duck pieces on hot platter surrounded by chestnuts. Spoon over yogurt sauce and serve at once. Serves 2.

## Pheasant Marsala

1 pheasant
¼ cup white wine
¼ cup butter
1 onion, finely chopped
1 cup yogurt
1 cup cooked pitted cherries, semi-sweetened
1 T Marsala
  salt
  pepper

Marinate cherries in Marsala for 2 hours. For basting sauce, saute onions in butter until golden; remove from heat; add yogurt and seasonings. Clean and split pheasant down the back. Sprinkle with wine and broil 30 to 40 minutes, basting frequently with yogurt sauce. Remove to a hot platter, serve surrounded with marinated cherries.

## Hasenpfeffer

2 rabbits, sectioned
1 cup wine vinegar
2 onions, sliced
2 onions, minced
1 clove garlic, minced
6 pepper corns
4 cloves
1 bay leaf
1 carrot, finely chopped
½ t tarragon
¼ t basil
¼ cup soft butter
1 cup yogurt
1 cup fine brown bread crumbs
    salt and freshly ground pepper

For marinade, mix in casserole all ingredients except butter, sliced onions, yogurt and bread crumbs. Marinate rabbit in cool place for 24 hours, turning several times. Dry sections. In a large skillet, saute rabbit in hot butter until browned. Add minced onions, brown lightly, then add 1 cup strained marinade. Cover and cook over medium heat until liquid cooks out. Add another ½ cup marinade and cook 10 minutes. Remove rabbit to warming oven. To juices in skillet add bread crumbs and yogurt, stirring until gravy thickens. Replace rabbit sections; mix well and serve. Serves 4 to 6.

## Wild Grouse Casserole

2 grouse with giblets
½ cup flour
¾ cup butter
¼ lb. ham, thinly sliced
4 shallots, finely chopped
1 clove garlic, minced
2 cups dry white wine
1 cup button mushrooms
1 T minced parsley
1 t basil
2 drops Tabasco sauce
1 cup yogurt
    salt
    pepper

Disjoint grouse and chop giblets. Rub grouse sections with salt and pepper; dust lightly with flour. Melt butter in a large skillet and saute sections and giblets until lightly browned. Line bottom and sides of casserole with ham and arrange grouse pieces on ham. To the skillet of giblets, add shallots and garlic; saute 2 or 3 minutes. Add 1 cup wine, mushrooms, parsley, basil and Tabasco; bring to boil and pour over grouse. Add remaining cup of wine and cook covered in 350° oven 1½ hours. Carefully stir in yogurt and return to oven for 5 minutes. Serves 2 or 3.

## Huntsman's Venison Chops

*6 venison chops*
*1 onion, sliced*
*2 carrots, sliced*
*4 shallots, chopped*
*4 sprigs parsley*
*½ t thyme*
*1 t salt*
*6 crushed peppercorns*
*6 juniper berries*
*½ cup vinegar*
*¼ cup olive oil*
  *red wine*
*¼ cup butter*
*1 cup yogurt*

Combine venison chops, vegetables, seasonings, vinegar, oil and enough red wine to cover chops. Let stand in refrigerator 24 hours. Drain, reserving one-half cup of marinade. Heat butter in large skillet and cook chops 4 minutes on each side or until done. Remove the venison to hot platter and keep warm. Add reserved marinade to skillet and bring to boil. Stir in yogurt and reheat. Serve sauce separately. Chops are excellent when served with wild rice.

## Oriental Duck

*1 duck, 4 to 5 lbs.*
*½ cup yogurt*
*2 t salt*
*1 t saffron*
*2 T oil*
*2 onions, finely chopped*
*5 cloves garlic, chopped*
*3 inch piece of ginger root*
*1 t ground dried chili peppers*
*2 bay leaves*
*3 cups boiling water*
*4 slices onion*
*2 T grated unsweetened coconut*

Cut duck into serving pieces. Coat duck with mixture of yogurt, salt and saffron. Let stand 1 hour. Heat oil in skillet and saute chopped onions and garlic until golden brown. Add ginger, chili peppers, bay leaves and duck. Cook for 15 to 20 minutes or until duck is brown. Remove excess fat and add boiling water. Cover and cook over low heat for 20 minutes. Add coconut; cover and cook for another 25 minutes, basting occasionally. Add sliced onions and continue cooking 15 minutes. Makes 4 servings.

## Liver Stroganoff

1½ lbs. beef liver,
  cut into 1 inch strips
2 onions, sliced
¼ cup oil
½ t salt
  pepper
½ lb. mushrooms,
  cleaned and sliced
1 cup hot water
2 T flour
1 cup yogurt
  pinch oregano

Saute onions and mushrooms in oil until tender. Add liver and brown lightly on all sides. Add salt, pepper and hot water; stir well. Cover and simmer over low heat about 15 minutes or until tender. Remove liver from skillet and keep warm. Mix flour and oregano with yogurt until smooth. Add ¼ cup mushroom sauce from skillet and blend smoothly with yogurt. Pour yogurt mixture gradually into skillet, mixing well. Cook over low heat, stirring constantly, until thickened. Add liver and reheat. Serves 6.

## Frankfurters Sauerkraut Casserole

12 skinless beef frankfurters
2 T oil
¼ cup chopped onions
2 cups sauerkraut
  water
1½ cups yogurt
1 T flour
1 T honey

Cut frankfurters in half and brown lightly in oil. Remove from skillet. Drain sauerkraut juice into a cup, adding enough water to make 1 cup of liquid. Combine yogurt and flour; mix until well blended. Gradually stir in chopped onions and honey to make sauce. Line bottom of a 1½ quart casserole with half the sauerkraut. Place half the frankfurters in a layer over sauerkraut, then pour half the sauce over it. Make another layer of remaining sauerkraut and top with sauce. Split the remaining frankfurters lengthwise and arrange over top of sauce. Cover and bake in 350º oven for 45 minutes. Remove cover for final 15 minutes. Serves 6.

# CHEESE & EGGS

## Quiche

1 cup mushrooms, sliced and drained
1 onion, thinly sliced
2 T melted butter
2/3 cup chopped Swiss cheese
½ cup chopped cooked ham
½ t salt
½ t white pepper
¼ t paprika
1 cup yogurt
5 eggs, well beaten
  pie shell, uncooked

Saute mushrooms and onions in butter. Spoon into bottom of pastry shell. Top with cheese and ham. Combine salt, pepper, paprika, yogurt and eggs. Beat with rotary beater until smooth. Pour mixture over cheese and ham. Bake in 400° oven 20 to 25 minutes or until mixture is set. Serve hot.

## Yogurt Cheese Souffle

1¼ cups yogurt
1 cup sifted flour
1 t salt
¼ t pepper
2 T chopped chives
½ cup grated Parmesan or
  Romano cheese
6 eggs, separated

Mix yogurt, flour, salt and pepper until smooth. Stir in chives and cheese. Beat egg yolks until thick. Gradually add to yogurt mixture, stirring constantly. Beat egg whites until stiff but not dry. Fold into yogurt-egg mixture carefully but thoroughly. Put into an oiled 1½ quart baking dish. Place in a shallow pan of hot water and bake in 350° oven for 1 hour or until set. Serve immediately. Serves 6 to 8.

## Corn Cheese Pie

1 9" pie shell
1 cup yogurt
½ t salt
½ green pepper, chopped
1 onion, chopped
¼ cup chopped parsley
2 eggs
2 cups corn, cooked
½ cup wheat germ
1 t basil
¼ cup grated cheddar cheese
2 T butter

Whirl all ingredients, except cheese, in blender. Pour into uncooked pie shell. Sprinkle with cheese. Bake until center is firm, about 10 minutes at 450º then about 25 minutes at 350º. Serves 6.

## Bulgarian Souffle

1½ cups yogurt
4 eggs
½ cup milk
½ lb. dry cottage cheese
¼ cup soft bread crumbs
1 T chopped chives or parsley
  butter
  salt and pepper

With an egg beater, blend yogurt until smooth; add eggs and continue beating until completely blended. Add milk, cottage cheese, and mix until smooth. Add bread crumbs, salt, pepper and herbs. Pour mixture in buttered baking dish. Bake in 400º oven about 40 minutes or until top is brown. This souffle may be served hot or cold as a main dish or as hors d'oeuvre. Serve 4.

## Vegetarian Kebabs

4 slices stale dark bread, cut in
  1 inch squares
2 egg yolks, beaten
1 green pepper, cut in 1 inch squares
½ lb. sharp cheese, cut in 1 inch cubes
¼ lb. cherry tomatoes
½ cup yogurt
  salt and pepper
  flour
  olive oil

Skewer cheese, tomatoes, green pepper and bréad alternately until all is used. Blend egg yolks with yogurt, salt and pepper. Dip each kebab into this mixture; sprinkle generously with flour and fry in hot olive oil until pale golden brown. Drain well before serving. Serves 4.

## Eggs Nested in Spinach

1 lb. spinach, chopped
1 onion, chopped
¾ cup yogurt
3 T butter
1 clove garlic, crushed
6 eggs
  salt and pepper

Wash spinach and cook in water that clings to the leaves. When spinach has wilted, remove from heat and drain thoroughly. Melt butter in a saucepan and saute onion until lightly browned. Salt and pepper and remove from heat. Mix the drained spinach and onions together and put into a shallow baking dish. Make a nest for the eggs in the spinach. Drop eggs into the nest. Mix yogurt and garlic; add a pinch of salt. Whip until smooth and spoon over the eggs and spinach. Bake in 375º oven until eggs are set. Serves 4 to 6.

## Turkish Poached Eggs

2 cups yogurt
1 small clove garlic, finely minced
1 t vinegar
2 T butter
6 eggs
  salt and pepper

In mixing bowl, beat yogurt until smooth, add garlic, salt and vinegar. Pour the mixture into a serving dish. Poach the eggs; drain and arrange in yogurt. Melt butter in a small saucepan and add paprika for color. Salt and pepper to taste. Garnish eggs with paprika butter and serve at once or place in 375º oven about 10 mintues to warm the yogurt. Serves 4 to 6.

## Omar Omelette

3 eggs, lightly beaten
2 T flour
1/3 cup yogurt
1 T minced chives
1 T butter
  salt and pepper

Add salt and pepper to lightly beaten eggs; whisk in the yogurt. Sprinkle flour over egg mixture and blend lightly but thoroughly. Heat a frying pan; add butter and pour in half the omelette mixture. Cook over low heat, moving the omelette around in the pan to avoid burning. When brown underneath, turn it, as you would a pancake. Cook the other side. Serve at once. Repeat with the remaining batter. Serves 2.

## Eggs Czarina

4 eggs
1 cup yogurt
4 slices dark bread
2 T butter
  salt and pepper
  minced parsley

Cut each slice of bread into a round. From the center of each round, cut out a small circle to form a thick ring. Saute rings of bread in butter. Place them in a buttered baking dish. Drop an egg into the center of each bread ring; season with salt and pepper. Top with yogurt. Bake in 350º oven until eggs are set. Serves 2 to 4.

## Eggs with Wine Sauce

2 shallots, finely chopped
1 cup button mushrooms
½ cup dry white wine
1 t chopped tarragon
½ cup yogurt
1 cup stuffed green olives
6 hard-cooked eggs, chopped
  salt and pepper

Saute shallots until golden brown. Cook mushrooms in small amount of water and add wine, tarragon and seasonings. Boil fiercely for 3 minutes. Add shallots and yogurt, stir well. Reheat. Pour wine sauce over chopped eggs and surround with olives. Serves 4 to 6.

# RICE, GRAIN & PASTE

## Yogurt Rice

*1½ cups yogurt*
*1 cup buttermilk*
*2 T minced green pepper*
*1 t salt*
*½ t grated ginger*
*1/8 t cayenne pepper*
*4 cups cooked rice*
*1 T oil*
*1 t mustard seed*
*1 bay leaf, crumbled*

Blend yogurt, green pepper, ginger, buttermilk, salt and cayenne. When thoroughly mixed, combine with cooled rice. Saute mustard seed and bay leaf in oil until seeds pop. Cool and stir into rice. Chill several hours before serving. Makes 4 to 6 servings.

## Yoghetti

*½ lb. spaghetti*
*¼ cup olive oil*
*6 oz. tomato paste*
*1 T butter*
*1 clove garlic*
*2 cups yogurt*
  *salt and pepper*

Drop spaghetti into salted boiling water. Boil until tender but not soft. Drain. Return to saucepan, add butter and toss lightly until spaghetti is well coated. In another pan, heat oil and saute garlic for a minute or two, then add tomato paste and seasoning. Remove from heat; add yogurt and blend thoroughly. Pour sauce over the hot spaghetti. Serves 6.

## Persian Rice

½ cup rice
3 cups water
3 cups yogurt, beaten
1 T flour
1 t salt

Soak rice ½ hour in 1 cup water. Add 2 cups water to yogurt; mix well. Mix flour with small amount of water to make a paste, then add to yogurt. Heat to boiling. Drain water from rice. Add rice and salt to yogurt. Cook over low heat for 10 minutes. Makes 5 cups.

## Macaroni and Cheese

2 cups elbow macaroni
½ lb. cheddar cheese, diced
¼ cup butter
  salt
  pepper
1 cup yogurt

Cook macaroni until tender. In 1½ quart casserole, place one third of macaroni and one third of cheese. Dot with butter, sprinkle with salt and pepper and add one third yogurt. Repeat layers until all ingredients are used. Bake covered in 350º oven for 30 minutes. Serves 4 to 6.

## Saffron Rice

1 cup yogurt
6 oz. chopped almonds
½ lb. long grained rice
1 egg
¼ t saffron
  butter
  salt and pepper

Rinse rice for 1 minute in boiling water and then drain. Drop the rice into fast boiling salted water and cook for 10 minutes. Rinse again, this time in cold water, and drain. Beat egg and mix with yogurt and half the cooked rice. Grease a casserole and put in yogurt rice mixture. Sprinkle with chopped nuts, then a layer of remaining rice. Repeat layers until all is used. Sprinkle with saffron, salt and black pepper. Bake in 375º oven for 40 to 50 minutes. There will be a crust on the bottom of the casserole. Turn upside down and serve with golden crust on top. Serves 4.

## Armenian Barley

1 cup barley
½ cup cooked chick peas
3 cups yogurt
1 t salt

Cook barley until well done; drain. Add chick peas and salt. To cooled mixture, add yogurt and blend thoroughly. Serve chilled. Makes 4 to 6 portions.

## Kasha

*2 cups buckwheat groats*
*3 T oil*
  *hot seasoned stock*
*1 cup yogurt*
*1 T soy flour*

Saute buckwheat in oil in top of double boiler over direct heat, stirring constantly. When all grains are coated with oil, add soy flour and enough boiling stock to cover buckwheat to depth of ½ inch. Cover and place over bottom of double boiler; cook gently over hot water until tender and stock has been absorbed. Add more stock if needed. Just before serving, blend in yogurt. Serves 6.

## Alpine Breakfast

*½ cup whole oats, raw*
*1 cup water*
  *juice of 2 lemons*
*½ cup yogurt*
*6 apples with skins, shredded*
*¼ cup honey*
*¼ cup finely chopped nuts*

Soak oats overnight in water. Mix oats with all other ingredients. Serves 4.

## Wild Rice and Mushrooms

*3 T oil*
*1 onion, sliced*
*½ lb. mushrooms, sliced*
*1 t salt*
*1 T minced parsley*
*1½ cups wild rice*
*2 cups boiling stock*
*1 cup sweet cider*
*¾ cup yogurt*

Wash rice in cold water. Heat oil; saute onions and mushrooms. Add salt, parsley and rice; stir until rice is coated with oil. Add 1 cup hot stock. Cover tightly and cook over low heat until liquid has been absorbed; add remaining cup of stock. When stock has been absorbed, add cider, continue cooking covered until cider has been absorbed and rice is done. Remove from heat and blend in yogurt. Serves 6.

# PANCAKES & BREADS

## Marble Coffeecake

1¾ cups sifted whole-wheat cake flour
1½ t baking powder
½ t baking soda
½ cup margarine
¾ cup sugar
2 eggs, unbeaten
1 cup yogurt
1 t vanilla extract
¼ cup sugar
2 t cinnamon
½ cup raisins
½ cup chopped walnuts

Sift flour with baking powder and soda. In a large bowl, cream margarine with sugar, then with eggs, vanilla, and yogurt until fluffy. Add alternately dry ingredients with yogurt mixture. For topping, mix ¼ cup sugar, cinnamon, raisins and walnuts. Pour half of batter into 9" x 9" x 2" pan; sprinkle with half of topping. Cover with remaining batter and top with balance of raisin mixture; press lightly with spoon. Bake 45 minutes in 350º oven. Makes 8 to 10 servings.

## Sunday Brunch Pancakes

6 eggs, separated
5 T raw sugar
1 cup yogurt
1 cup milk
1 cup flour
½ cup corn starch
4 t baking powder
½ t salt

Whip together egg yolks and sugar. Add milk and yogurt and blend until smooth. Sift flour, measure; sift again with cornstarch, baking powder, and salt. Combine with yogurt mixture. Mix well, beat egg whites until stiff, and fold in. Bake on a medium hot griddle. Serve with melted butter and yogurt topping, or your favorite syrup. Serves 6.

Yogurt Topping: Mix 1 to 2 T honey to 1 cup blueberry or boysenberry yogurt. Other fruit flavored yogurt may be used.

## Wonderful Waffles

2 cups sifted flour
3 t baking powder
1 t baking soda
1 t salt
2 cups yogurt
4 eggs, separated
1 cup melted butter or margarine

Heat waffle iron. Sift flour, baking powder, soda and salt together. Combine yogurt, butter and beaten egg yolks; add to flour mixture and mix at high speed until smooth. Beat egg whites stiff and fold into batter. Bake in waffle iron. Reheat iron before pouring in next waffle. Makes 6 to 8 waffles.

## Onion Bread

1 package active dry yeast
2 T warm water
2 t sugar
1 cup scalded milk
½ cup butter
1½ t salt
3 cups flour
5 large onions, sliced
2 eggs, beaten
½ cup yogurt
4 slices bacon, cooked and crumbled
1 t caraway seed

Soften yeast in warm water with sugar. Pour milk over ¼ cup butter and 1 t salt. When lukewarm, add yeast and flour. Mix well. Cover and let stand in warm place until double in bulk, about 1 hour. Punch down and knead until smooth. Roll out and press into a 10" x 15" x 1" greased pan. Cook onions in remaining butter until tender, but not brown. Cool and stir in ¼ teaspoon salt, eggs, yogurt, bacon, and caraway. Spread evenly on the dough. Let rise until light, about 30 minutes. Bake in 400º oven for 30 minutes. Cut in squares and serve hot. Can be reheated if wrapped in foil.

## Indian Fried Bread

3 cups whole-wheat flour
1 t salt
½ cup butter
1½ cup yogurt

Mix well and knead until smooth. Form balls, then roll into thin flat cakes. Fry in deep fat at 380º until puffed and brown. Serve at once.

## Whole-Wheat Wafers

1½ cups whole-wheat flour, sifted
1 t salt
½ cup yogurt

Blend flour and salt. Gradually work in yogurt to make dough. Knead on lightly floured board for about 15 to 20 minutes. Roll until tissue thin and cut into small strips, squares or diamonds. Place on oiled cookie sheet. Prick with a fork. Bake for 10 minutes, until lightly brown, at 350º. For variation; add cumin seed, caraway seed, dill seed or sesame seed.

## Rice Cakes

1 egg, beaten
2 T margarine, melted
1 cup cooked rice
1½ cups yogurt
1 cup flour, sifted
2 T sugar
½ t salt
¾ t soda
½ cup milk

Mix egg, yogurt, margarine and rice in a bowl. Add sifted dry ingredients and milk. Stir until well mixed. Spoon onto hot lightly oiled griddle, turning to brown on both sides. Serve with favorite syrup or plain. Makes about 18 3" cakes.

## Yogurt Dough Biscuits

*2 cups flour, sifted*
*2 t baking powder*
*½ t soda*
*1 t salt*
*¼ cup shortening*
*¾ cup yogurt*

Sift dry ingredients. Cut in shortening with a pastry blender until mixture resembles coarse corn meal. Stir in enough yogurt to make a soft dough. Turn out on floured board. Roll out until dough is ½" thick. Cut with biscuit cutter and bake on greased baking sheet in 450º oven for 12 to 15 minutes.

## Irish Soda Bread

*4 cups sifted flour*
*¼ cup sugar*
*1 t salt*
*1 t baking powder*
*2 T caraway seeds*
*¼ cup butter or margarine*
*2 cups raisins*
*1 1/3 cups yogurt*
*1 egg*
*1 t baking soda*
*1 egg yolk or a little cream*

In mixing bowl, sift flour, sugar, salt and baking powder; stir in caraway seeds. With pastry blender or 2 knives, scissor-fashion, cut in butter until coarse like corn meal; add in raisins. Combine yogurt, egg and soda; stir into flour mixture until just moistened. Turn dough onto lightly floured surface; kneed lightly until smooth; shape into ball. Place in greased casserole. With sharp knife, make 4 inch cross, ¼ inch deep in top center. Brush with egg yolk. Bake in 375º oven 1 hour or until done. Cool before slicing.

## Banana Bread

*2 cups sifted flour*
*1 t soda*
*1 t baking powder*
*½ t cinnamon*
*½ t nutmeg*
*¼ t salt*
*1 cup mashed bananas*
*2 eggs*
*1 cup sugar*
*¼ cup yogurt*
*¾ cup chopped walnuts*
*1 T melted butter*

Sift together flour, soda, baking powder, cinnamon, nutmeg and salt. In mixing bowl, beat egg slightly and add bananas and sugar. Beat until smooth and stir in yogurt; add dry ingredients. When blended, stir in nuts and butter. Pour into greased 9 x 5 inch loaf pan. Bake in 350º oven 1 hour or until toothpick comes out clean. Cool to room temperature; wrap in waxed paper. Chill. Serve thinly sliced.

## Sundowner Corn Bread

*¾ cup yellow corn meal*
*1 cup unsifted flour*
*½ cup sugar*
*2 t baking powder*
*½ t baking soda*
*½ t salt*
*1 cup yogurt*
*¼ cup milk*
*1 egg, beaten*
*2 T margarine*

Mix all ingredients just enough to blend. Pour into greased pan and bake in 425º oven about 20 minutes. Cut in squares, serve hot with butter.

# DESSERTS

**Magic Carpet**

*1 cup yogurt, drained*
*¼ cup raspberries*

Mix yogurt and raspberries well and chill. Serve in dessert glasses and sprinkle top with a bit of orange blossom honey.

**Apricot Whip**

*1 package dried apricots*
*1 or 2 T honey*
*1 cup yogurt*
*1 cup water*

Wash apricots and soak over night in water. Put apricots with juice in blender, add honey and whirl until smooth. Pour mixture into a bowl and whip in yogurt with a fork. Serve chilled. Makes 4 servings.

**Strawberry Creme**

*1 cup heavy cream*
*½ cup milk*
*½ cup sugar*
  *dash of salt*
*1 envelope unflavored gelatin*
*¼ cup cold water*
*1 cup yogurt*
*2 T brandy or strawberry liqueur*
*2 cups strawberries, crushed and*
  *honey sweetened*

Combine cream, milk, sugar and salt in a saucepan. Cook over low heat until sugar is dissolved and remove. Soften gelatin in cold water and stir into the cream mixture until gelatin is dissolved and then let cool. When cool, beat in yogurt until smooth. Add flavoring. Pour into individual molds and chill until firm. Unmold and serve with crushed strawberries. Makes 4 to 6 servings.

## Spiced Apples

1 lb. cooking apples
¼ cup brown sugar
1 t cinnamon
¼ cup port
6 T butter
¼ cup yogurt

Core and slice apples thickly. Cook slices in hot butter, stirring continuously until soft and golden brown. Add sugar, cinnamon and port; cook 5 minutes more. Remove from heat and fold in yogurt. Spoon into sherbet glasses and serve hot or chilled. Serves 4.

## Danish Raspberry

2 t fresh lemon juice
2½ cups red raspberries, crushed
¼ cup honey
2 T butter
1 T flour
¼ t salt
1½ cups milk
¾ cup yogurt

Mix lightly lemon and raspberries. Chill. Melt butter in saucepan and add flour. Blend in honey and salt; add milk, stirring vigorously. Cook over moderate heat until thickened, stirring constantly. Cool. Refrigerate until well chilled. Just before serving, fold together raspberries and yogurt. Add to the chilled mixture, stirring until smooth. Serves 6 to 8.

## Almond Ice Cream

1 envelope unflavored gelatin
1 cup pineapple juice
1 cup orange juice
  juice of 1 lemon
1½ cups honey
1½ cups drained yogurt
½ t almond extract
¼ t salt
½ cup toasted slivered almonds
1 cup heavy cream, whipped

Set refrigerator control for coldest setting. Sprinkle gelatin on pineapple juice in saucepan. Add honey and heat, stirring until gelatin is dissolved. Cool. Add orange and lemon juice. Blend yogurt with almond extract, salt and almonds. Stir in first mixture and fold in whipped cream. Pour into freezing tray and freeze until firm. Serves 6 to 8.

## Avocado Ice Cream

1 large avocado,
  peeled and seeded
1 cup yogurt
½ cup powdered milk
¼ cup honey
1/3 cup lemon juice
  rind of 1 lemon

In blender, mix all ingredients until smooth. Freeze in freezing tray. Stir 2 or 3 times during freezing.

## Peach Ice Cream

*2 cups sliced fresh peaches*
*1½ cups yogurt*
*4 T honey*
*1/3 cup orange juice*

In blender, whirl all ingredients at low speed until smooth. Pour into freezing tray. Beat once or twice while freezing to prevent ice crystals from forming.

## Orange Sherbet

*2 cups orange juice*
*2 t unflavored gelatin*
*  rind of 1 orange*
*1½ cups drained yogurt*

Soften gelatin in ½ cup orange juice and heat until dissolved. Cool by adding remaining orange juice and orange rind. Pour into freezer tray and freeze slowly to a soft mush. Add yogurt and beat until smooth. Return to freezer and freeze only to a firm texture.

## Mango Freeze

*1 cup mango pulp and juices*
*3 T honey*
*1 cup yogurt*

Choose large ripe mangos. Cut the pulp away from the seed into a mixing bowl, then mash. Add honey and yogurt. Taste and add more honey if desired. (Mangos vary in natural sweetness). Mix well and place in refrigerator ice tray to freeze. It is not necessary to beat. The mango mixture will become hard and firm, but will not turn to ice. Remove from refrigerator and allow to soften to desired consistency before serving.

## Dessert Rum Souffle

*3 cups yogurt, beaten*
*¼ cup cream*
*¼ cup flour*
*¼ cup butter*
*4 eggs, separated*
*½ t cream of tartar*
*½ cup sugar*
*2 T rum*

Melt butter in saucepan and blend in flour. Add yogurt and cream; mix well and cook over low heat, stirring constantly, until thick and creamy. Remove from heat. Beat egg yolks until thick and lemon colored; add sugar and rum gradually and stir into yogurt mixture. Put egg whites in a bowl with cream of tartar and whip very stiff. Fold egg whites into batter. Pour into a 2 quart souffle dish; set in a shallow pan of water and bake about 50 minutes in 325º oven until golden. Serve immediately with rum-flavored whipped cream. Makes 4 to 6 portions.

## Poppy Seed Cake

*2 cups rice flour*
*¾ cup poppy seeds*
*1 cup yogurt*
*¾ cup oil*
*1½ cups brown sugar*
*2 t baking powder*
*¼ t soda*
*  pinch salt*
*3 egg whites, beaten stiff*

Soak poppy seeds in yogurt for 3 hours. Blend oil and brown sugar; add to yogurt. Sift together rice flour, salt, baking powder and soda. Mix dry ingredients with yogurt mixture and fold in beaten egg whites. Pour batter into two cake pans which have been lined with waxed paper. Bake in 350º oven for 30 minutes.

## Orange Bundt Cake

*1¾ cups flour*
*1 t baking powder*
*1 t baking soda*
*1 cup raw sugar*
*1 cup butter or margarine*
*3 eggs, separated*
*1 cup yogurt*
  *grated rind of 1 orange*

Cream butter and sugar. Add egg yolks, yogurt and orange rind; beat until light and fluffy. Sift together flour, baking powder and baking soda. Stir into yogurt mixture. Fold in egg whites which have been beaten until stiff but not dry. Turn into oiled and floured bundt mold. Bake at 325º for 1 hour. Remove from oven and let stand for 10 minutes. Loosen carefully around edge and turn out on plate with a rim. Pour hot orange syrup over top of cake slowly so cake will absorp syrup evenly.

## Orange Syrup

Combine juice of 2 oranges, ¾ cup of raw sugar, juice of 1 lemon and a dash of salt. Boil 3 or 4 minutes. Pour hot over cake.

## Mt. Olympus Sundae

*1 cup yogurt*
*1 to 2 T honey*
*2 T chopped almonds*
  *pitted date*

Put the yogurt in a chilled sherbet cup. Pour honey evenly over yogurt; sprinkle with chopped nuts and top with date. Makes 1 large sundae.

## Lemon Pound Cake

*6 eggs, separated*
*¼ t cream of tartar*
*2 cups raw sugar*
*1 cup butter or margarine*
*2 t grated lemon peel*
*2 T lemon juice*
*3 cups flour*
*1 t soda*
*¼ t salt*
*1 cup yogurt*

Beat egg whites with cream of tartar until soft peaks form. Gradually beat in ½ cup sugar until foam is stiff and glossy; set aside. Cream together butter and remaining sugar. Add egg yolks one at a time, beating after each yolk. Blend in lemon peel and lemon juice. Sift flour, measure 3 cups, and then sift again with soda and salt. Add flour mixture alternately with yogurt and butter mixture. Mix batter until smooth and fold in egg whites. Pour into a well greased and flour-dusted 10 inch tube pan. Bake in 350º oven for 60 minutes or until tooth pick inserted in the center comes out clean. Cool 10 minutes in pan, then turn out on wire rack to cool. Dust with powdered sugar before serving. Makes 12 servings.

## Slim Shortcake

*1 angel food loaf cake*
*1 cup crushed strawberries,*
  *honey sweetened*
  *strawberry yogurt*

Slice angel food cake into individual servings. Top each piece with strawberry yogurt and crushed berries. Variation: Any other fruit and yogurt.

## Strawberries Romanoff

*1 qt. strawberries*
*¼ cup honey*
*1 cup vanilla yogurt*
*1 cup heavy cream*
*¼ cup Cointreau*

Wash and hull berries; coat with honey. Chill at least 3 hours. Just before serving, whip cream until stiff. Beat yogurt smooth and fold into whipped cream. Fold in Cointreau and strawberries, reserving a few to put on top of mixture. Serve at once. Makes 6 to 8 servings.

## Raspberry Angel Cake

*2 cups sifted flour*
*1 t baking powder*
*1 t baking soda*
*½ t salt*
*¼ cup butter*
*1 cup raw sugar*
*1 egg*
*1 t vanilla*
*1 cup raspberry yogurt*

Sift flour, soda, baking powder and salt. In a large mixing bowl, cream butter with sugar until fluffy; beat in egg and vanilla. Stir in flour mixture and yogurt alternately until blended. Spoon in greased 9 inch angel food tin. Bake in 350⁰ oven for 50 minutes, or until wooden toothpick inserted near center comes out clean. Cool upside down for 10 minutes, then loosen around edge and center with a knife. Turn out on rack and let cool thoroughly. Dust with powdered sugar. Serve plain or with a large scoop of raspberry yogurt.

## Carob Cake

*½ cup margarine*
*¾ cup dark brown sugar*
*2 eggs*
*1 cup sifted whole wheat pastry flour*
*½ cup carob powder*
*1½ t cinnamon*
*½ t baking powder*
*½ t baking soda*
*½ t salt*
*½ cup yogurt*
*1 t vanilla*

Cream margarine and sugar. Add eggs and beat well. Combine all dry ingredients and sift together three times. Add sifted dry ingredients to creamed mixture alternately with yogurt, beating until smooth and creamy. Pour in to oiled 8" x 8" baking pan; bake at 350⁰ for 25 to 30 minutes. Cool and frost with Carob Fudge Frosting. Makes 1 layer.

## Carob Fudge Frosting

*1 cup dark brown sugar*
*2 T carob powder*
*1/3 cup rich milk*
*2 T butter*
*1 t vanilla*

In a saucepan, combine sugar, carob powder and milk. Cook over medium heat to soft ball stage when tested in cold water. Remove from heat, add butter and vanilla. Allow to cool to lukewarm, then beat until thick.

## Coconut Cream Pie

1 baked pie shell
1 cup yogurt cream cheese
2/3 cup yogurt
2 T honey
1 t vanilla
1¼ cup shredded coconut

Blend together yogurt, yogurt cream cheese, honey and vanilla. Fold in coconut, reserving 1 tablespoon for topping. Pour into pie shell; top with remaining coconut and chill until set.


## Almond Yogurt Pie

2 cups yogurt, beaten
3¼ cups farina
1 t baking soda
2 t baking powder
2 cups raw sugar
½ lb. coarsely chopped almonds
2 T grated orange peel

In a bowl, mix farina with soda and baking powder; add yogurt, sugar, almonds and orange peel. Mix well for 2 or 3 minutes. Pour batter into a well-greased baking pan and bake 30 to 40 minutes in 350º oven. When done, remove from oven and pour lemon syrup over the top. Allow pie to cool before serving.


## Lemon Syrup

1¼ cups raw sugar
1 cup water
1 T freshly grated lemon peel

Boil water and sugar in a saucepan 5 minutes. Add lemon peel and pour over pie while hot.


## Cream Cheese Pie

1 baked pie shell
1 T unflavored gelatin
¼ cup cold water
2 egg yolks, beaten
¼ cup milk
1 cup yogurt
1 8 oz. package cream cheese
¼ cup honey
1 t grated orange rind
1 t vanilla

In double boiler, mix gelatin and cold water. Heat until gelatin dissolves. Blend egg yolks with milk and add to gelatin. Stirring constantly, cook over gently boiling water until mixture coats a silver spoon. Cool. Cream honey, cheese, vanilla and orange rind. Add yogurt and continue mixing until smooth. Slowly stir in cold gelatin mixture. Chill for about 20 minutes, then beat until creamy smooth and pour into a nut or coconut pie shell. Refrigerate to set.


## Coconut Pie Shell

1 cup coconut
2 T butter

Mix butter and coconut, pack into an 8 inch pie pan. Bake in 350º oven until edges brown. Cool before filling.


## Nut Pie Shell

1 cup ground almonds or other nuts
2 T sugar
1 T butter

Mix nuts, butter and sugar; form into a pie shell. Toast in a moderate oven or serve raw. Cool shell before filling.

## Spicy Raisin Pie

½ cup raw sugar
2 T cornstarch
½ cup corn syrup
½ t salt
1 t cinnamon
¼ t nutmeg
¼ t cloves
2 eggs, separated
1 cup yogurt
1 cup raisins
1 baked pie shell
1/8 t cream of tartar
  pinch salt
4 T sugar

In top of double boiler, mix together sugar, cornstarch, syrup, salt, cinnamon, nutmeg and cloves. Beat egg yolks and add to mixture. Stir in yogurt and raisins. Cook over hot water until thickened, about 20 minutes. Pour into baked pie shell. Beat egg whites until foamy, then beat in cream of tartar and salt. Add sugar a tablespoon at a time. Beat until stiff peaks form. Top pie with meringue. Brown in 350° oven.

## Strawberry Cream Pie

1 8 inch pie shell, baked
1 cup yogurt, drained
1 8 oz. package cream cheese
3 T honey
½ t vanilla
1 cup sliced strawberries

Combine yogurt, cream cheese, 1 tablespoon honey and vanilla. Beat to the consistency of whipped cream. Pour into baked pie shell and refrigerate until set. Before serving, top with strawberries which have been sweetened with 2 tablespoons honey. Variations: Use peaches, blueberries, papaya or favorite sliced fruit instead of strawberries.

## Spiced Apple Pumpkin Pie

1 envelope unflavored gelatin
¼ cup water
2 cups cooked pumpkin
½ cup honey
1 t cinnamon
½ t ginger
¼ t cloves
½ t salt
2 cups spiced apple flavored yogurt
1 9 inch pie shell, baked

Sprinkle gelatin on water in saucepan and heat until dissolved. Set aside. In a mixing bowl, blend all other ingredients, except yogurt. Add whipped yogurt and gelatin. Again, mix until smooth and creamy; pour into pie shell and refrigerate until set. Just before serving, decorate with whipped cream and sprinkle with chopped nuts. A nut crust is very tasty with this pie.

## Creme Louisa

1 cup heavy cream
½ cup sugar
½ cup milk
  dash salt
1 envelope unflavored gelatin
½ cup cold water
1 cup yogurt
½ t almond flavoring or 2 T brandy
  or strawberry liqueur
  crushed strawberries, sweetened with honey

Combine cream, milk, sugar and salt in suacepan; cook over low heat until sugar is dissolved. Remove from heat. Soften gelatin in cold water and stir into cream mixture. When gelatin is dissolved, beat in yogurt with rotary beater, only until thoroughly blended. Stir in flavoring and pour into individual molds. Chill until firm. Unmold and serve with berries. Makes 4 to 6 servings.

## Spicy Cupcakes

2 T soft butter
½ cup sugar
1 cup yogurt
2 eggs, beaten
1¾ cups flour
1 t baking powder
¾ t soda
½ t salt
½ t cloves
½ t cinnamon
¼ t nutmeg
1 T grated orange rind

Cream butter and sugar until fluffy. Beat in yogurt gradually. Add eggs, salt and orange rind. Sift flour, soda, baking powder and spices twice, then add to batter, stirring only enough to combine. Fill oiled cupcake moulds half full and bake in 375° oven for 20 minutes or until toothpick inserted in cake comes out clean. Makes 18 cupcakes. Variation: Add 1 cup currants or ¾ cup chopped nuts.

## Cossack Cheese Patties

2 cups cottage cheese
1 cup yogurt
  honey
  chopped nuts

Drain cottage cheese and yogurt overnight or until all whey drains off. Shape into patties; place on oiled cookie sheet. Bake at 200° until patties are dry and firm. Cool; top with honey and sprinkle with chopped nuts. Delicious served with fresh fruit.

## Devonshire Pears

1 can (1 lb. 13 oz.) pears
  juice 1 orange
  juice 1 lemon
¼ t ginger
1 stick cinnamon
3 whole cloves
½ cup currant jelly
  red food coloring
1 cup heavy cream
½ cup yogurt
2 T honey
1 t vanilla extract

Drain pears, reserving syrup. In saucepan, mix syrup with orange and lemon juice and spices. Let stand 1½ hours. Add pears and simmer until thoroughly heated. Cool, then chill. Beat jelly until smooth. Add small amount of red coloring and 3 tablespoons liquid from chilled pears. Remove pears to serving dish and cover with jelly mixture. Whip cream until stiff. Fold in remaining ingredients and spoon in a circle on pears. Serves 8.

## Baked Bananas Caliph

6 bananas
8 oz. cream cheese
4 T butter
4 T brown sugar
1 t cinnamon
1 cup yogurt

Cut bananas in half lengthwise and brown lightly in butter. Put 6 banana halves in buttered baking dish. Cream sugar, cinnamon and cream cheese; spread half mixture over bananas. Add another layer of bananas and spread with balance of cheese mixture. Top with yogurt and bake 20 minutes in 375° oven. Serves 6.

## Date Dreams

¼ cup margarine
¾ cup brown sugar
1 t vanilla extract
1 egg, well-beaten
1½ cups sifted flour
½ t soda
¼ t baking powder
¼ t salt
¼ t cinnamon
1/8 t nutmeg
½ cup yogurt
2/3 cup chopped dates
36 walnut halves

Cream together margarine, sugar and vanilla. Add egg and mix well. Sift together dry ingredients. Add to creamed mixture alternately with yogurt. Stir in dates and drop teaspoon of mixture onto greased cookie sheet. Top each cookie with a walnut half. Bake in 400° oven about 10 minutes. Makes 3 dozen cookies.

## Black Strap Cookies

3½ cups sifted whole-wheat pastry flour
1 t baking powder
1 t soda
1 t salt
2 t cinnamon
1 t ginger
½ t cloves
¾ cup oil
½ cup black strap molasses
¾ cup honey
1 egg
¾ cup yogurt

Sift and mix together flour, baking powder, soda, salt and spices. In a bowl mix oil, egg, molasses and honey. Blend thoroughly and alternately add the flour mixture and yogurt. (Chopped raisins may be added if desired). Drop from a teaspoon onto a greased baking sheet. Bake in 375° oven for 12 minutes or until done. Dust with powdered sugar. Makes several dozen cookies.

# BEVERAGES

## Guru's Goblet

*½ cup grape juice*
*1 cup apple juice*
*2 T yogurt*
*¼ cup raisins*

Mix all ingredients in blender until smooth and creamy. Serve in goblet or stemmed wine glass. Makes about 2 cups.

## Date Shake

*1 cup yogurt*
*1 cup milk*
*4 ice cubes*
*1 small ripe banana*
*6 pitted dates*
*2 T honey*
*4 almonds*

Whirl all ingredients for 2 minutes in a blender. Serve in chilled glasses.

## Abdug

*This drink is very common in Persia.*

*2 cups yogurt*
*½ t salt*
*2 cups ice water*
  *mint sprigs*

Whirl yogurt, salt and ice water in blender for about 2 minutes. Serve in tall chilled glasses and garnish with sprigs of mint. Ideal for hangovers.

## Spicy Lassi

*Lassi is a yogurt drink from India.*

*2 cups yogurt*
*4 cups water*
*¼ t salt*
*½ t ground cumin seed, roasted*
  *pinch cayenne*

Whirl all ingredients in blender for about 1 minute. Chill well.

### Creamy Apricot Nectar

*1 cup apricot nectar, chilled*
*1 cup yogurt*

Blend and serve in chilled glasses. Variations: Try raspberry, orange, concord grape, pear, peach, strawberry or pineapple juice. Sweeten with honey to taste.

### Red Eye

*1/3 cup yogurt*
*2/3 cup beat juice*
  *pinch dill*

Blend all ingredients well and serve in chilled glasses. Makes 1 cup.

### Summer Peach Drink

*1 cup fresh, sliced peaches*
*1 cup yogurt*
*1 cup skim milk*
*2 T honey*

Place all ingredients in blender and whirl until smooth. Makes 3 cups.

### Cinnamon Prune Juice

*1½ cups prune juice*
*1½ cups yogurt*
*¼ t cinnamon*
*1 T lemon juice*
*1 T honey*

Mix all ingredients in blender until smooth. Makes 3 cups.

### Bloody Mary

*½ cup yogurt*
*½ cup tomato juice*
  *salt and paprika*

Whirl all ingredients in blender for about 30 seconds. Serve chilled.

### Strawberry Cooler

*1 cup sliced strawberries*
*1 cup yogurt*
*1 cup skim milk*
*2 T honey*

Whip all ingredients in blender until smooth. Makes 3 cups.

### Strawberry Fizz

*1 cup sliced strawberries*
*1 cup club soda*
*1 cup yogurt*
*2 T honey*

Mix in blender until smooth. Makes 3 cups.

### Raspberry Refresher

*1 cup raspberries*
*¼ t anise seed*
*1 cup yogurt*
*1 cup skim milk*
*2 T honey*

Press raspberries through a food mill or wire strainer; discard seed. Blend raspberry pulp with all other ingredients. Makes 3 cups. Blackberries may be used instead of raspberries.

## Cornucopia Cocktail

*1 cup pineapple yogurt*
*1 cup milk*
*1 cup fruit cocktail*
*4 ice cubes*

Combine all ingredients in blender. Mix well and serve in chilled glasses. Makes 3 cups.

## Pineapple Shake

*1 cup pineapple juice*
*1 ripe banana*
*1 cup pineapple yogurt*
*6 ice cubes*

Whirl all ingredients in blender at high speed for 2 minutes. Makes about 4 cups.

## Polynesian Pick-Up

*1 cup papaya juice*
*1 cup yogurt*
*2 T finely grated coconut*

Whirl in blender until smooth. Makes 2 cups.

## Sweet Lassi

*2 cups yogurt*
*2 T honey*
*4 cups water*
  *pinch nutmeg*
  *pinch of cayenne to sharpen flavors*
  *dash rosewater*

Whirl in blender until smooth and serve chilled.

## Orange Caesar

*1 cup plain yogurt*
*1 cup orange yogurt*
*1 cup orange juice*
*2 T coconut*
*2 T honey*

Mix all ingredients in blender until smooth. Chill and mix again just before serving. Serves 3 or 4.

## Table of Equivalents

| | |
|---|---|
| dash or pinch | Less than 1/8 teaspoon |
| 3 teaspoons | 1 tablespoon |
| 2 tablespoons | 1/8 cup |
| 4 tablespoons | 1/4 cup |
| 5 tablespoons +1 teaspoon | 1/3 cup |
| 8 tablespoons | 1/2 cup |
| 10 tablespoons +2 teaspoons | 2/3 cup |
| 12 tablespoons | 3/4 cup |
| 16 tablespoons | 1 cup |
| 1 cup | 8 fluid ounces |
| 2 cups | 1 pint (16 fluid ounces) |
| 2 pints | 1 quart (32 fluid ounces) |
| 1 quart | 4 cups |
| 4 quarts | 1 gallon |
| 16 ounces (dry measure) | 1 pound |

## Can and Jar sizes of Canned Foods

| Approximate Net Weight or Fluid Measure on Can Label | Approximate Equivalent in Measuring Cupfuls |
|---|---|
| 8 oz. | 1 cup |
| 10½ to 12 oz. | 1¼ cups |
| 12 oz. | 1½ cups |
| 14 to 16 oz. | 1¾ cups |
| 16 to 17 oz. | 2 cups |
| 1 lb. 4 oz. or 1 pt. 2 fl. oz. | 2½ cups |
| 1 lb. 13 oz. | 3½ cups |

## Abbreviations

cup . . . . . . . . . . . . . . . . . . . . cupful
lb. . . . . . . . . . . . . . . . . . . . pound
oz. . . . . . . . . . . . . . . . . . . . ounce
pt. . . . . . . . . . . . . . . . . . . . pint
qt. . . . . . . . . . . . . . . . . . . . quart
T . . . . . . . . . . . . . . . . . . tablespoon
t . . . . . . . . . . . . . . . . . . . . teaspoon

## Oven Temperatures

250º up to 325º . . . . . . . . . . . . . . . . . . . Slow oven
325º up to 375º . . . . . . . . . . . . . . . . . . Moderate oven
375º up to 425º . . . . . . . . . . . . . . . . Moderately hot oven
425º up to 475º . . . . . . . . . . . . . . . . . . . . Hot oven
475º up to 500º . . . . . . . . . . . . . . . . . . Very hot oven

# INDEX

113

# NOTES